Acting by Mistake

Acting by Mistake

William Roudebush

To order additional copies of this book, contact:
Xlibris Corporation
1-888-7-XLIBRIS
www.Xlibris.com
Orders@Xlibris.com

Contents

For Denise,
All of my students,
And Julia Cameron

FORWARD

The first thing I hope for Bill Roudebush's book is that it's printed in a light volume. That way, it will be easier for me to carry around when I go away to act a role, when and if that happy situation arises. It will be easier for all the actors who will want to take it with them, and I think there will be a lot of those.

The ideas in this book have been licking around the edges of my teaching, acting, and when I have the nerve to let it, my directing. For several years, I've only been partially able to articulate, or utilize, what Bill's book, and his teachings have brought right out into the middle of things, where I have begun to believe they belong, and with blazing clarity.

I'll try to tell you how I got started with some of these ideas: In 1993, at Playwrights Horizons, in NYC, I had the great fortune to act in a brilliant play by Jonathan Marc Sherman, called "Sophistry". In my opinion, it is one of the best plays of the 90's, and is published by Dramatists' Play Service. It was directed by Nicholas Martin and had a wonderful cast, which included Ethan Hawke, Calista Flockhart, Steve Zahn, Anthony Rapp, Linda Atkinson, Nadia Dajani, and Mr. Sherman himself. I thought, I must,somehow not mess this up for myself. One does look back and remember all the opportunities, and the ways they could have been more, well....seized! So I thought, what if I try something I've never before tried as an actor? What if I try not to have an opinion of my work, in this play? I trust Nicky Martin to have an astoundingly accurate opinion of it, so why do I need to have one? I remember the times I'd thought I was absolutely brilliant, and it was more or less forcibly brought home to me, that maybe I was not! I also remember all the times I thought I was lost, and it was suggested to me that I was actually found. Here is where we get into the real territory of Bill's book, because the suggestions made to me I always forcibly resisted. It was obvious to me, that when I had an opinion of my work, it had often been wrong! So why not just not have one?

Well, it helped. There were more nights than usual when I was, as they say, in the moment. Something began to stir. That SOMETHING is the crucial something that Bill describes so well. I've been struggling to understand it ever since "Sophistry", and tried to carry what I learned in that play to other plays by Shakespear, Wendy Kesselman, Warren Leight, Don DeLillo, and other richly challenging writers. Cobwebs of my old opinions have continued to cling to these attempts, but fewer all the time. Bill's book is going to make them fewer still. It's going to help you too. I think I can promise that. Have a wonderful time with it!

Austin Pendelton

INTRODUCTION

Acting is something I love. I love to observe it, mostly. I've been directing plays for about thirty years now, so I believe I'm a qualified observer. I've watched actors suffer, struggle, intellectualize, stew, stop, re-start and soar above the audience's heads. It's been a joyous run of talent that has passed before my eyes and taken me around the block more than once.

I started as a technician who watched actors do things I could only dream about. I remember, after deciding I wanted to study theatre, transferring to the University of Miami in Florida. Soon, I found myself sitting in the Ring Theatre watching auditions for Brian Friel's *Philadelphia Here I Come*. I was eighteen and scared literally stiff as I watched these actors audition. They were all so good. One was Bert Park's son, Joel. He eventually was cast as Gar Private. I had already filled out an audition card and was sure they were going to call me next. Cringe. Pause. No, not this time, but certainly next. This went on for about an hour and a half until my name finally rose to the top. The monitor calls, "Bill Roudebush." Frozen, I was frozen. Again, "Bill Roudebush." I relaxed as the first creative thought of the evening flashed into my consciousness. If I remain silent my audition will soon be over, I thought. One more "Bill Roudebush" and my audition officially concluded. I sat anonymously in my seat for a moment, then crept out, unseen, during the next break.

I was a sophomore and just transferred from another school.

No one knew me. I eventually ended up a light board operator and began my acting "career" from a tiny glassed-in booth. Fear. Life's biggest block. Nothing creative can happen when it is present. Nothing happened that fateful audition night. Nothing happened for many years to come because of that Rock of Gibraltar in my path—my own fears. You have to go through it. Some of us have to go through it for decades and some of us will continue for decades to come. It's a powerful force.

Each of us has our own definition of fear, so I went immediately to *Webster's Dictionary* to lay it out on the table. Webster spends almost half a page on the topic, so I'm going to do some editing and focus on its direct applications to acting. Fear:

1. *A feeling of anxiety and agitation caused by the presence or nearness of danger, pain, etc.*

    This is what I'm referring to when I say that fear blocks creativity. When we sense the "presence or nearness of danger," everything is blocked because all your energy becomes immediately focused on that presence. This book will prove to you that no danger is actually present. Basically, I'm going to transfer this useful energy into character, and literally mask your perceptions out of the entire process.

2. *Dread; terror; fright; alarm, panic, and dismay*

    These synonyms pretty much sum up the acting experience.

A. *Dread refers to the depression felt in anticipating something dangerous or disagreeable (to live in dread of an audition)*

    The key word here is anticipation. When you anticipate, your energy becomes result-oriented. If you are pursuing an acting career for results, you may as well close this book right now.

B. *Terror applies to an overwhelming and often paralyzing feeling (I live in terror that I will forget my next line.)*

    There are endless applications for this word. I have felt this along with each one of you. Time and experience, will enable you to work through this crippling block and challenge it's existence in your process.

C. *Fright* applies to a sudden, shocking, usually momentary feeling. (When they asked me for a second monologue it gave me a *fright.*)

We all expect things to go a certain way. We are usually frightened by change, but change is where creativity in acting becomes engaged. I will show you that fright in acting is the fuel that ignites your imagination and challenges your perceived limitations. If you don't expect anything, you cannot be frightened.

D. *Alarm* applies to a sudden realization of danger. (He felt *alarm* when he went up on his next line.)

Alarms go off in the head of almost every actor. "Did I say that right?" "Why is that other actor pausing so long? Have they forgotten their line?!" "What's my cue?!?" Most actors have a running monologue about the events of the production that lives outside the context of character and play. I will give you methods that can completely eliminate this useless running commentary from your process.

F. *Dismay* implies a loss of courage or a feeling of consternation at the prospect of trouble or danger. (He felt *dismay* over his continued lack of success at auditions.)

This, to me, is the most daunting of all fears. If you are losing courage it means that, at one time, you actually had it. Actors frequently continue in the craft because they love it and are encouraged by others whom they respect. Often progress moves quickly and a new self-confidence is obtained. Things seem bright, prospects are hopeful, and setbacks seem impossible. Setbacks will occur and it is how you face them that will define you as an artist. I will offer you insights that will keep your disappointment from turning into dismay.

So taking all these definitions, synonyms and ideas into account there is one thought I want to place into your acting process wherever it may be in its development:

The only mistake you can make, as an actor, is to be afraid to make a mistake. Fear is the only obstacle you must overcome.

Once removed, all things become possible. The actor must deal with this every day. Remember your first improvisation? The cold fear? I remember mine. Buckets Lowery's acting 201 class at the University of Miami, 1967, "Okay . . . you're a pillar on the Greek Parthenon . . . the sun is beating down on your stony façade . . . you're objective is to . . ." I think I stopped listening with the word, 'pillar.' What could I do? How can I be a pillar? What does everyone think I will do? What can this teacher mean? How can he do this to me? Why me? "Why me?" I learned that in high school. It's in my yearbook. It was one of my "sayings" so you can tell I've had this victim mentality entrenched in my buried imagination for years. The exercise? It was a disaster. And Buckets was not shy about relating that fact to me. This was 1967. Before Oprah, when everyone just said what he or she felt. No apologies and, it seemed, very little compassion. I began my exploration of acting with this huge ice block of fear that refused to melt until I had directed well over fifty productions.

Directing is where I really learned to act—by observing. It's safer than doing. Doing means exposure-of myself. Observing is something you can do for years and never get caught. That observation is where most of the ideas for the following text originated. I have acted but I was always working to get so lost in the act of acting that I couldn't learn anything. I became a director, stepped outside the process and saw it clearly like so many different pieces of clothing worn on other people. One thing I know for certain is the only mistake you can make is to be afraid to make a mistake: Hence "Acting By Mistake."

Where to Use Your

Imagination

Very recently an amateur actress came up to me to report her homework. She was a middle-aged woman who was also a painter. She had a twelve-line part in a play I was directing and was having trouble making a human connection to her lines.

I had worked privately with her for about two hours on these twelve lines and we were beginning to make progress. She began to realize that the thought behind the line was more important than the line itself. This particular day she was very proud of the fact that she had done a great deal of homework the night before. "Bill," she said, "I worked all last night using my imagination with this character's thoughts, I tried to be as creative as possible. I think I really know what I am going to do out there tonight." I paused without saying a word. She sensed that somehow I wasn't completely pleased with her focused study and asked me what was wrong. I felt her dismay, so I immediately replied that nothing was wrong and I was encouraged that she took so much time out of her schedule to work the part.

My hesitation was due to the fact that I didn't want her to show me what she worked on last night. Planning imagination or planning a creative approach is not useful in acting; planning, in fact, is the least desirable form of creativity for an actor. "You mean I shouldn't have worked on it last night?" She asked with a slight quiver in her voice. "No," I said, "I couldn't be more pleased that you did. I just don't want you going into rehearsal showing me what you created last night. If it's really valid it will reappear during tonight's rehearsal without you showing me. If your creation is valid you can forget about it. If it is endemic to the character it will surface without conscious thought. The place to use your imagination is tonight. Listen to what the other actor is saying to you, just as you are listening to me this moment. Really hear it. Take that line into your character. Once you've actually done that, make up your character's reply in that instant." The actor only has that tiny moment, between hearing what is said and making their scripted reply, to create. That is the only moment that counts, and that is where the actor uses imagination in their work.

Homework is great. Making decisions at home is great. Knowing your lines and what you think you want to do to them is great! When you come to rehearsal put all that work where it actually is—behind you. If it is really part of the scene it will make its appearance. Use your homework to completely trust yourself so you can actually listen to what's going on right now. Study hard. Work hard. Work hard, so you know you have the tools available to create something that is based on what is actually happening. You must know it so well that you can re-invent it on the spot. Planning your creativity puts it in a can. It is counterproductive. It is born in fear. The fear of not being creative . . . so obviously, I will plan it and it will be creative. Do you see that it is a fear-based solution?

Thank you for working so hard! Keep it up, but when you come to rehearsal forget your homework and focus on the work that is being created right in front of you. That is where your imagination is of greatest use to you. Let your creative homework fuel a fearlessness during today's rehearsal. Trust yourself knowing how hard you've worked. Trust yourself so much that you can forget about what your imagination so carefully planned last night. You will make mistakes rehearsing this fearless instinct and those mistakes will be your guide for tomorrow's homework. When you come to rehearsal, practice using your imagination in the moment and, by the time you get to performance, your imagination will be trained to create something fresh every night.

Using Acting By Mistake

Use this when you walk on the stage to *rehearse*, when you walk onto the stage to **audition** or when you walk onto the stage to **perform**. This is a focus guide for high-risk situations. This is not an acting technique, but it applies to every technique you already employ.

There are two important aspects to the development of an actor's process. First, you have to find the character, know everything about the character, feel the character, empathize with the character . . . I could go on forever and so should the good actor always continue to accumulate knowledge of who you are becoming. Stanislavski, Boleslavski, Strasberg, Adler, Meisner, Hagen, any of the great teachers can give you ideas for how to know a character and their needs. This is your homework and the more you invest the more complete your character will become. Do this at home. Imagine their past. Find their passions and get an image of who they are. Do your research—work patiently at home! BUT, when you come to work with other artists in rehearsal, performance and auditions you must leave your homework at home. That's why it's called homework!

In Rehearsal

Rehearsals are not homework. They are a laboratory for failure. They are where you begin the process of committing yourself to what is going on in the character's world this moment. Every rehearsal, just like every performance and audition, is different. It's the second week of rehearsal and everyone's trying to get off book. You're halfway between what you want to know and what you do know. You're working through a difficult scene with another actor. They forget their line. Everything stops. Usually the actor apologizes, "I'm sorry." Sometimes it's "expletive deleted!!" Occasionally, it's a grunt or a scream but always it stops the rehearsal process. The actor begins beating him or herself up and takes all others present out of the flow of the scene. That actor is not rehearsing. That actor, and I'm sure that actor is you, is trying to get it right. Rehearsals are not for getting it right. Rehearsals are where you try to connect to the impulse of a scene, listen to the other actors and explore the moments that are unfolding right in front of your eyes. So, everything stops. Someone announces the correct lines and the scene begins again, but not really . . . how can you re-connect to everything that was flowing so well before? It's not possible.

The rehearsal has been interrupted by a line mistake. An actor made a mistake. Big deal! That's what rehearsals are for! The more mistakes you make the less you are trying to get it right, which you can't do anyway because you are halfway between what you do know and what you want to know. You punish yourself, the other actors and the flow of the scene with this heart-felt apology. It makes no sense! Wouldn't it be more constructive, when you come to this pause of not knowing your next line, to hold the energy of the character's present moment, call "line," still holding onto all that energy, listen for the line (still holding), receive the line and follow through back into the scene with that new information? This way you are learning the impulse of the scene and continuing the flow that helps all your collaborating actors follow through with their impulse. You've taken a negative line mistake which you knew you were going to make anyway and turned it around to a positive.

There's more . . . the mistake is good! Why? . . . because it shows you where you have to focus your studying tonight so you don't make the same mistake when you hit this point in the re-hearsal tomorrow. No negatives! Embrace your mistakes in rehearsals. They are your guides to study, research and total commitment to the moment. That's how rehearsals are best used; to rehearse commitment, not to get it "right" or "perfect." You could only do it once, so what's the point? You can't precisely repeat every moment, so why spend your time trying to do the one thing you can never do?

There's still more . . . let's say you make a mistake and a moment you never thought of before implodes into the scene because of this accident. This happens all the time during a film shoot; someone is shooting a scene, an unexpected event occurs but the actor doesn't stop the action. The actor uses the mistake to stumble onto a new thought that the writer or director never even thought of before. Now it's on film. The camera doesn't miss a trick. It's brilliant and preserved forever on celluloid. The director beams, the writer is overwhelmed, the critics praise this as the most in-spired moment of acting in the entire history of the cinema. It was a mistake! Mistakes are called genius on film but live actors in the rehearsal hall sit there and bemoan the fact that a line was missed, misquoted or mispoken. Rehearsals are for creating. The essence of creation lies in turning mistakes around to your advantage.

In Auditions

You've all sat waiting for an audition. If you haven't yet, you will. Look at the other actors. What are they doing? Well, one person is in a corner of the room, their face jammed against the corner, running lines over and over again. They believe it's a warming up technique. They think that running their lines will prevent a line mistake when they get in front of the audition inquisition. What they are really doing is stoking up their nerves . . . and God forbid they should forget a line during this rapid-fire review. A panic that makes the plague seem like the common cold begins to inhabit the body. There is no cure, and in the next instant, the monitor calls their name. Now our panicked actor must enter the audition with this doubt forefront in their mind. The audition will look like nine out of ten of all the other auditions that morning: self-conscious, fearful, unimaginative, canned, overly formal and disconnected. Then, when the actor leaves, having brilliantly remembered the forgotten line, they take with them the false satisfaction of having done well because they remembered the lines!

There is another actor who is running over the 'moments' of their monologue in another corner of the room. This actor knows the lines. The lines are not an issue here. They prepared for this audition with a coach last night and "nailed it" several times. The coach even remarked, "if you do it just like you did now during that audition tomorrow, you should get the part." That's what this actor is doing in their corner; re-creating those moments that were so effective last night. They drill over and over recalling precisely, meticulously what worked so effectively last night. That is what is taken into today's audition. They emerge from the audition feeling satisfied, even empowered by the fact that they remembered all the "moments." Truth be told, this actor looked like nine out of ten other actors who auditioned that day, stiff, formulated, nervous and uninspired.

These are fear-based activities layered onto the fearful dilemma of the audition itself. If you don't know the lines when you get to the audition you shouldn't be at that audition. You are unprepared. Lines are a basic issue, and if you are dealing with basic issues in the waiting room you should exit now. Running your lines over and over when you know your lines is even worse. You are doubting your own accomplishment each time you run over them. If you have taken the time to prepare yourself, trust the time you have spent.

Think of an audition as a storm; let's call it a hurricane. A category five, because this audition is extremely important to you. If you are in the storm, you are in one of two places. The windy place of turmoil, blowing, tumbling around with no point of reference. You see everything flying around with you, out of control in a state of disarray because of your juxtaposition. The other place is the *eye* of the storm. It's calm there. The sky is blue and if you look carefully, you can see things blowing *around* you, but you are stable, centered, and calm in the knowledge that you have prepared yourself for this important day. If the other actors are caught up in the fierce winds you have escaped then sit back, relax and enjoy the show. Pick up a magazine, bring your favorite book and think about the life that surrounds your character's monologue. Trust the fact that you are well prepared and ready to take your leap of faith in the audition itself. The other actor who did so well last night with the coach needs to relax too. They already know that they are not going to forget their lines. The time spent with a coach has prepared them in the best possible way. Trust the fact that the work is done. You have worked out with a trained professional and are prepared to create whatever happens today. Don't put your focus on specifically what worked so effectively in yesterday's coaching session. That was yesterday so leave it in the past. Today, the day that is actually happening, is different. You're different. The room is different. The entire situation has changed. Why spend your energy trying to do the one thing you're incapable of doing? You can't re-create yesterday's moments. Believe in yesterday's workout. Trust your work so much that you can re-invent it in today's world. Preparation should eliminate doubt, not fuel it. Have the courage to forget the things you are so desperately trying to hold on to.

The only mistake you can make when you walk into that audition is to be afraid to make a mistake. You can't protect yourself with yesterday's success. You can't limit yourself to yesterday's accomplishments. Re-invent yourself each day with your accumulated knowledge. The more important the audition, the greater the risk you should take. Even if you forget your line or miss a moment you are still better off than trying to repeat. Repetition is common, ordinary and sealed in a can. Repetition is what every one else is doing and, if you do it too, you will look like everyone else. If you ever get an opportunity to audit a full day of auditions from the other side of the table, take it. You will observe and it will open your eyes to what I am telling you.

Here's a short story for your comfort. I have taught many audition classes. At the end of each ten-week session I would invite a local artistic director and do a mock audition—but it wasn't always so mock. Usually the guest artistic director was looking for early career actors and I was not shy in telling my students they could possibly get work out of this mock exercise. I wanted them to be nervous. During class time we had become bonded; supportive of each other's work and this is a good thing, not tonight, however. Tonight I wanted to see how students react to pressure rather than support.

The class begins. The students collect in the theatre lobby

while my guest and I arrange ourselves in the stage house. We begin and all seems to be going well. I'm learning a great deal about each of my students in the new light of tension. In walks a young actor, does his introduction and begins his first of two audition monologues. He gets four lines into it, extremely well connected, speaks the fourth line and our guest director bursts into laughter at the truthfulness of his delivery. The actor pauses, then goes blank. He turns to our table and apologizes for his mistake. Our guest is still laughing but suppresses it to say, "That's fine. Don't' worry. I really enjoyed what you have shown me so far. Why don't' you take a moment and do your second monologue." The shocked actor regroups and begins again. He does a yeoman's job and turns to say thank you, when our guest says, let's go back and try that first one again. He complies. He gets to the fourth line, delivers it with aplomb and our guest explodes with laughter again. My student goes blank once more. There's a pause as the laughter clears, the actor apologizes again and retreats to the lobby with his creative tail between his legs.

We then see six more student auditions and my guest director turns to me and says, "Can I keep this picture and resume?" He was, of course, referring to the student who couldn't get through both monologues. The student who forgot his lines. Every other student in the class got all their lines correct, but the one who made the brilliant, well-connected mistake got noticed.

My point: take the risk of making a mistake. Directors aren't looking for those who get it right. They are looking for those who are connected to what's happening in today's moment; Whatever that may be and however brief it may be. As an actor you will never know what a particular director is searching for, so focus your energy into the one thing you have control over—you. Stop protecting what should be and work with what is actually happening.

In Performance

When you step out onto the stage opening night, or any other night, for that matter, trust the number of hours you have rehearsed to get you to this point. Just because there is an audience watching doesn't mean you are suddenly responsible for getting it all right. You're not going to . . . so don't put your energy into something you can't do. Open up. Don't close down. Use what you have learned in those impulse refining rehearsals to take you where tonight leads you.

Have you ever run a show for more than thirty performances? What was the difference between the first show and the thirtieth? Confidence. You have succeeded twenty-nine times, so you know you are going to succeed. Why can't you feel that way opening night? . . . Because you're afraid of making a mistake. You're on guard. You're protecting your own imagination. You're shielding your own creativity. You have been rehearsing for weeks. Trust that time. There are other actors to make up a stroke for you if you should miss one. You're safe. Don't limit yourself by trying to get it right. Take that bungee leap of faith—especially on opening night. Your cord won't snap and you might actually enjoy the ride. Incorporate what you have learned in rehearsal to make you fearless in performance. The only mistake you can make tonight, any night, is to be afraid to make a mistake . . . and you probably will. But be assured you will not make that same mistake again . . . you will continue to learn, and the process continues as your vision opens up to what is actually happening . . . you invent with each new performance.

Then there's the story of the actor who, during first preview in front of an audience, gets a huge laugh on a line he didn't realize was the least bit funny. It empowered him. It was a total accident. No one, including the director or writer, expected it. So he goes out the next night and does it again—same reaction. The play continues to run but by the end of the second week, he was no longer getting that same laugh that ambushed everyone during previews. Then he thinks, "It must be the way I'm delivering it." So the next night, a new delivery, but still no reaction. The following night, yet another variation—still no laugh. He was desperate by now. What happened?

What changed was that he was now going out each night expecting a reaction. He was looking for the anticipated jolt of laughter. I must tell you that almost every great reaction an actor receives should be a total accident. Expectations on the stage kill the life of the moment. Whatever is actually happening out there is being put on hold while the anticipated laugh line is being delivered. Eventually, if this continues, the whole reason for the laugh is being pre-empted by the expectation of its arrival.

Each night of performance should be like a rehearsal with a huge energy source in attendance. You should, as in rehearsal, go out there to connect with what is actually happening during that performance. If the audience reacts, great! Use their reaction to fuel what comes after but don't anticipate anything. Learn to trust what is present. Words like expectation and anticipation are fear based and can only, if continually practiced, lead to disappointment and disillusionment. If I expect something and it doesn't occur all that remains is an empty consciousness. When I anticipate laughter and there is silence I begin to focus on myself. What's wrong with me? What's wrong with the audience? Both of these feelings are destructive and they take me out of the play. Nobody wins. Each performance is a well-rehearsed accident. You know what is going to happen but it has never happened exactly this way before. Accidents, by definition, are surprises and being surprised is what will always make an audience laugh.

Then there's the actor who has done fifty performances and is 'phoning' this one in. The play is a hit and this unconscious stupor comes over the actor's psyche. "Here we go again. I can't wait until the matinee is over. If I have to say this line one more time I think I'll scream." I want to pull that actor off the stage. Nothing is more annoying. When the production is successful and this apathy sets in my ire doubles.

Every new performance should be an exciting adventure. Use what you have learned from each previous performance to open your vision wider. You can now see things you have never seen before. Incorporate the advantages of accumulated experience. If you don't enjoy this process, get off the stage and let someone who is passionate take over. Don't waste an opportunity. Re-invent yourself each night your confidence builds. The more you absorb the richer your performance will be. When that process stops for you it's time to move on to the next project.

What You Must Do

In order to begin to touch some of the concepts outlined in this book there is one requirement. Ultimate knowledge. You must really know your lines. They must become second nature.

I once directed a musical review called *Tomfoolery*. I directed this five times during a five-year time span. There is a number in that show called "The Elements." It is simply a list of the chemical elements set to the tune of "Modern Major General." It is an awesome task of line memorization to undertake. While rehearsing this song with five different actors over that five-year period I ended up learning the impossible lyrics myself. Not the tune, but each one of the one hundred and three chemical elements. I can knock them off in less than forty-five seconds to this day. My point is, I don't have them memorized. I have ultimate knowledge of them. If I had them memorized I couldn't rattle them off so quickly. By the time I remembered what was next I would have been at least three elements behind in rapid-fire rhythm. You must know the lines to your monologue or scene this well.

Lines should never be the issue. When you focus on the lines you are living in a lifeless dimension. With ultimate knowledge you are in total control of that character's life. You now have that life force energy available. Give yourself the opportunity to access this force. Without this basic commitment to change, the principles of *Acting By Mistake* cannot be touched.

Actors do many erroneous things to protect their knowledge

of the lines. These are not character actions, pauses or hesitations. They belong solely to the actor. The only way to remove these false blocks to creativity and connection is to have ultimate knowledge of the lines. Get it done. This way you can use and focus your energy on what is happening to the character in the moment. This is your basic job. Do it well and do it first so you can move on to the real work that lies before you.

Don't do it unless you must

This is the best advice you can give someone who is trying to become an artist. If there is the least bit of drudgery attached to any part of the process a red flag should go up. It should get your attention. You should deal with it, nurture it and develop a strategy. Find a way to turn this negative force into fuel. Ask people. Talk to yourself. But deal with it.

Don't bemoan a negative. That's what everyone is doing. That's one reason, in an audition, you look and sound like everyone else. They are unhappy about some aspect of their process too, but they are brushing it aside because they need this job. The job becomes more important than the process. It just doesn't work as effectively in that order.

The love of the entire process is what makes the true artist/ actor rise to the top. If something bothers you discover what it is. If you know, deal with it. If you need help, get some. If you are still burdened begin to search for something in your life that is void of this self-doubt and drudgery. The more you are afraid the more you will put it aside and the less chance you will have to eradicate it from your process.

The jobs are more likely to come if you focus on your process with each new audition instead of the result. You will get more laughs if you stop playing for them. The drama of a character's dilemma will be deeper if you stop being dramatic.

A Grain of Truth

The whole process starts from the smallest place. When we think about the truth of ourselves it lives in a protected cavern. It seems minuscule, yet it encompasses our point of view, experiences and all our feelings. It is the place every character that really lives on stage protects with all their being. It is the most intense center of activity in our body.

Intensity is the key. When creating a character we usually begin in the wrong place. We start by talking out loud. Reading the lines. Most of us begin to perform on the first reading of the script. It is our natural tendency to do this. We are going to, one day, after weeks of rehearsals, perform this play, so naturally we start to create the performance with performance energy. We begin projecting the character before we really find the character and this energy of projection can distort the truth of the character. Once we begin this projection process it rarely gets smaller. The character's life and the actor's needs get intrinsically locked together. That small place where the character lives, silently, quietly, frequently afraid and often intimidated gets buried in this process.

When I see an actor disconnected from the character's center I try a grain of truth exercise. I have them work on their monologue or scene in a small place. They whisper the lines and transplant that projection energy into the tiny place where the character lives. If it's intense, that's all right. Intensity can be as quiet as a fuse burning before a bomb explodes. If the character is crying or even wailing, that external symptom is germinated in the deepest center of the character's soul. If the character is joyful, that bliss is born in the seeds of the character's existence. It all begins there. That's where you can start to know your character. Begin your relationship in a quiet place. Don't project anything yet. Once you discover some truth then you can enlarge it to fit any occasion and the size will always be born in that discovered truth. This gives you more freedom than ever, because no matter how BIG YOU MAKE IT, the truth will always be present. Once you find the truth, all the performance energy in the world can't bury it. Projection will, in fact, enhance it.

I learned this several years ago when I was rehearsing a new play at the Mint Theatre Company in New York. We were about to open in one week. We were at the point of run-throughs in the rehearsal process. There was another show running in the adjacent room and the walls were paper-thin. This usually wasn't a problem, because we rehearsed during the day while the production performed nightly. However, because of schedule conflicts, we were forced to do a night rehearsal simultaneously with the performance play. It seemed impossible, but we found a way to turn it around to our advantage. We had a whisper through. I told all the actors I wanted them to rehearse at full impulse, but contain that impulse in the smallest place. They were not allowed to project. I wanted them to inject their projection energy into the intensity of the character's intent, action and objectives. "Hold nothing back," I told them; only your vocal energy and don't hold that back either. Transplant that energy towards the character's center. It was the most creative rehearsal the company had experienced and it led to expansive realizations for the remaining rehearsal period . . . just start with a grain of truth.

Stop Listening to Yourself

How did you do? "I did great! I did everything I have been working on. I really nailed it!" These are comments actors make that are big indicators to me. What they indicate is that the actor really didn't do well. How could they? They were listening to themselves and when that is happening you can never be at your best.

Artistic brilliance has nothing to do with consciousness. Genius is an accident. Ask any artist, athlete or scientist, for that matter, to analyze or explain a moment of invention or perfection and they can't. It just happens. The moment emerges from a complete investment of your accumulated knowledge that is heightened by an inexplicable inspiration. The intellect has been overridden by involvement and imagination.

Einstein's theory of relativity flashed into his mind during a completely unrelated conversation. Picasso's invention of cubism accidentally emerged from a sketch, a doodle on a piece of scrap paper. Their consciousness wasn't present, something else was, something that can't be defined, let alone analyzed.

Think of it this way. You have one hundred percent. All your energy can only be one hundred percent of yourself, your entire being. Now in the locker room scene of some "B" movie, a coach can be demanding one hundred and ten percent of his players, but the truth is they only have one hundred percent. All of yourself is quite a lot and none of it should be wasted listening or monitoring yourself. It's just less energy for the character and, in a perfect world, we want a transformation. Nothing is more counter-productive to this transformation process than standing outside of your own being and charting your progress. That single activity requires a tremendous amount of energy, and what that energy is doing is splitting your focus. It is fear-based. We feel it necessary to check out how we are doing moment to moment, because we are afraid of making a mistake.

This self-examination is the only thing you can possibly do wrong. It's counterproductive. It's not possible to do both things well simultaneously, and the math doesn't even add up. When I spend forty percent of my energy listening to myself, I've just made it impossible to inject one hundred percent into the character. This is another reason that nine out of ten actors look alike in an audition. They are all doing the same thing; thinking, listening and checking their progress during the event itself.

Acting is a very self conscious art form, so your natural human tendency is to monitor yourself at every juncture. You simply want to do your best. Don't beat yourself up for engaging in this activity. Begin a process to eradicate your self-monitor. Imagine what you can do with this newfound energy. Begin to take the first steps towards unconscious acting; acting based on trust in yourself, confidence and the instinct of the moment.

How do you get rid of these voices in your head? You know, the ones that are saying, "Oh, you missed that beat change! You said that word wrong! What am I doing up here? What's my next line?!" It's another monologue, isn't it? Think about it. You're really doing two monologues at the same time. Now that takes talent. If you can do this, and people say you are a good actor, just imagine what they will think when you are focused on one monologue.

How to Begin

Tell a story; a story that actually happened to you. If you're too self-conscious, get a friend and listen to a story they tell. Observe them carefully. What's the process of each moment as it occurs to them? You will see very little acting unless your friend knows what you are doing or they are extraordinarily histrionic. What you will most likely observe is a series of visions that lead to dialogue. The visions are the actual experiences of the story.

If you can't observe it, try it yourself. Describe in detail, your day today. You will find a sequence of pictures that were your activities. Your dialogue will come from these visions. This is where your focus lies. You're not worried about how you sound or how to interpret, or where to pause. Your focus is on composing the words that describe and clarify your specific experience. That should be your focus while you are doing a monologue. What happened to the character? Give yourself the character's experiences, and then recall the dialogue from the visions you've created. This will keep you occupied and the voices will be unable to intrude on this new focus. Each time you work, add more detail to the visions. Build your experience and speak from these refined visions of the character's life events. That's what we do in real life, so implant knowledge into your character.

For the sake of a working example I'm going to use Joanne's monologue to her close friend Sissy from the play *Come Back to the Five and Dime Jimmy Dean, Jimmy Dean.*

Sissy: O.K., I'm warned. What the hell were you doing in Oklahoma City anyhow?

Joanne: Actually, I went there with the intention of seeing you . . . I had heard you were living there and thought I'd show up on your doorstep. And surprise you . . . but, somewhere around the city limits, I lost my courage and ended up in some downtown bar instead . . . I'd had one or two drinks and was up on this platform leaning on the jukebox singing a song along to some record that was playing . . . you remember, like we used to . . . the record plays and you move your mouth and pretend you're Eydie Gorme.

Sissy: You can move your mouth and pretend all you want 'cause you don't know crap from Christmas.

Joanne: We'll see. Anyhow, there I was, singing away to myself when I glanced over the crowd and floating over a cloud of cigarette smoke was this face . . . a face from the past that jumped out to jar loose a whole lot of locked up memories. He sure was giving me the once over. His eyes were glued to my boobs just like the first time we encountered each other. He smiled that big dumb smile of his and came over to the jukebox . . . Said he had to tell me how much he loved my singin' . . . That I sounded just like Eydie Gorme. He invited me to join him for a drink, which I did . . . bourbon and water, wasn't it Sissy? Well that one led to another, and another and then he began to pour out the woeful tale of the wife he left behind him, the "Ex-Queen of the Dixie Roller Rink" from McCarthy, Texas who had boobs the size of watermelons. He really thought she was "something". . . thought so since their high school days when they'd get together for "hanky-panky" in the old graveyard. He was crazy over them watermelons of hers . . . They really won her over. They got married eventually and were living happily ever after, until . . . one day the watermelons just disappeared . . . Went away, and . . . so did . . . I'm sorry Sissy I went too far.

Now if I had to learn this monologue and I might, I could actually play Joanne because she is a transsexual whose alias is

Joe. I would start with the pictures of my experiences that day. It might go something like this: I remember coming into Oklahoma City to visit you-Sissy but (since you wouldn't recognize me anyway because of my sex change) I chickened out and ended up at this sleazy bar. I remember standing by the jukebox singing to an Eydie Gorme song (that was ironic because all of us girls used to do that when we were younger, even when I wasn't one of the girls). Anyway, this guy came over and brought back a flood of memories. The bar was very smoky and through the smoke he told me how much I sounded like Eydie Gorme but he couldn't take his eyes off my boobs. He bought me a drink and then another, and another and told me this woeful tale of the girl he fell in love with from McCarthy, Texas. The "Queen of the Roller Rink" with boobs the size of watermelons. How he would fool around with her in the graveyard at night and they eventually got married and one day he came home and the watermelons were gone . . . disappeared, just gone away—

I just wrote that stream of consciousness monologue from the pictures that came into my head. I only read the monologue once but I was focusing on the event rather than the actual lines. As I continue to refine my pictures I will develop the exact language of the playwright but my monologue will always come to me as pictures from the actual night Joanne spent in Oklahoma City when she didn't have the courage to visit her old friend Sissy. I can never go up on the event—I can't forget the event because the memory of it is where my process began. I may forget a word or two but never the event because I learned it through the pictures of the experience. If I were to re-read the monologue a second time and do the same exercise again there would be more detail in my memory. If I read it four or five times over the exact detail of the event would emerge. I would be adding more of the character's detail and the author's actual words. But my focus as the actor would always be the memory *not* the consciousness of how I am supposed to interpret it.

This is also a process where improvisation can be very constructive. Many character speeches, especially monologues, are based on information that occurs off stage or outside the dialogue of the play. Get some of your fellow actors and improvise the offstage experience so you are now recalling actual events that you have been involved with. If your character had an episode at the zoo, park or anywhere accessible to you, journey there and give your character the benefit of your observations. Now, when you work on your monologue, these visions will begin to permeate your process. Trust your knowledge of the lines and focus on the visions that inspire their specific composition.

Using the same example from *Come Back to the Five and Dime* . . . have your other cast members improvise the scene in the bar. Bring in another actor to play Sissy's ex-husband. Play an Eydie Gorme tune and sing to it. Have other cast members smoking and dancing to the music. Create the atmosphere and improvise the content of the monologue. Now when you recall the monologue you will be recalling an actual event that happened to both the actress *and* the character.

If you still hear these annoying voices in the background, get your characters emotional state involved. When you are saying anything, you also feel a certain way. This feeling pervades and encompasses your being. It's something happening to you that you can't control. Add this to the mix while recalling the visions, because they are directly connected. Using Joanne's speech as an example once again . . . Joanne is not reliving this monologue as so many actors might approach it. All the events she describes happened to her but the memory of those events is not what drives the speech. Her emotional survival is at stake in this monologue. She is being mocked. She is being blamed for something she had no part in. She is being accused of lying by a group of people who live their entire life as a lie. She has taken all that she is going to take. She is emotionally poised to tell a truth that, in any other set of circumstances, she would keep to herself. She must say what she has to say but she knows it will cause deep hurt. She is struggling with her own character's fight for survival and dignity versus the feelings of her deluded friends. This fight becomes where you place your focus. Couple that with recalling the visions of your character's experience, and the voice in your head will be obliterated by your character's present tense action.

I was working with a student just a few days ago. We have been working together weekly for almost a year. She has made huge leaps, but this particular day she was listening to herself. She had become so proficient at recalling all her character's experience that she had energy left over to listen to herself. So I asked her one question. "How does your character feel?" "Furious," she replied without hesitation. "She is furious, because she is being asked to do something she won't do. She is being asked to pretend that she is more 'nuts' than she actually is for the benefit of a judge that is reviewing her case."

Now, furious is a general term, so we discussed what this specifically meant to her. "Well," she said, "It's like when my kids have been told over and over not to do something, yet they continue. I feel betrayed to the point that I am almost speechless with fury." Now we were getting to something she had a direct relationship with. "That's perfect," I said, "now put yourself in the state of speechless fury and, as you recall the character's visions, try to keep from losing your temper or indicating just how angry you actually are. Whatever you do, hang on to that fury that encompasses this moment. Fight your character's feeling of betrayal and clarify what must be said in order to survive this outrageous situation she has been forced into." She did, and all the listening stopped. She was so active dealing with this new element that she had no energy left to listen.

You must give yourself character activities to focus on. You can't just say, "I can't listen to myself." Your mind and imagination are not structured to work with negative requests. If you tell yourself not to do something that's all your mind will focus on— what you don't want! Keep adding character details until your mind is too busy to listen to your voices. Your character's emotional state, past activities and present tense action should be the core of your process.

Don't listen to yourself. Speak from the memory of the character's experiences and present tense emotion—just like you do every day of your life.

Go Alone

When you go to an audition, go by yourself. The more important the audition, the more reason to go by yourself. Auditioning is the most difficult part of the entire process. It is an open opportunity for self-doubt. When you throw someone else into the mix it diffuses your focus.

The ride to the audition. Your friend is nerve racked and you're trying to stay centered or vice-versa. Either one is a negative. When you're centered and your friend is nervous, you try to calm them down. Now you lose your centered focus, or even worse, catch your partner's anxiety. Okay, you're nervous and your friend is totally focused. This begins a new process of self-doubt magnified by your omnipresent instability. "Why is she relaxed and I'm not? She is so calm . . . she must be better prepared than me. What is wrong with me?" . . . And so on.

Don't mix your energy with the others at the audition. Keep your own vigil. I don't mean, run off in some corner—just don't get involved. Watch, listen, observe, converse, but don't get emotionally involved. Encourage others but hold on to your focus. During the audition, if you are in a position to hear or watch, try to move to a different location. Acting is not a competitive sport. How others do should have absolutely no effect on you. How others perceive what they do is even more irrelevant. Don't hide, but don't get emotionally involved. Mixing your energy can only dilute your own solution.

Now there is the ride home. She was asked to do a third

monologue and you were not. She was told how right she is for so many things in the season. You received an encouraging nod. She can't stop talking about how much they loved everything she did. There you sit listening, growing smaller and smaller with each passing mile of this endless journey.

When you go to an audition, work on what you have control over: your audition process. Leave any result out of it. When you bring a friend, it instantly becomes a competition for results that will destroy your focus and resolve. Take risks. Take trust. Take the self-confidence you deserve for being prepared. Don't take a friend.

Remove Your Protections

We all want to be safe. In life, unless we feel safe, it is nearly impossible to create anything. When safety is the first concern, and it usually is, very little else matters until security is re-established. This is also true for actors. Fear is the most cumbersome block to remove. It can take a lifetime. Of course there are those who never feel it at all. The charmed ones for whom everything comes easily. Forget about them. Like Mozart or Einstein, they exist with these extraterrestrial or past-life instincts that we mortals can only be suspicious of. Work on yourself. Let go of the competition.

It's not easy to let go of fear as an artist, because we are exposing so much of ourselves for public scrutiny, but fear is the one thing we must work to eject from our process every day. It is so engrained in our being that our body and mind employ counterproductive behaviors to keep us safe. I call these activities protections. They must be removed one by one because, although they keep us safe, they act as a translucent barrier or screen which masks your uniqueness.

Almost everyone has protections they are unaware of. Our experiences, habits and lack of self-trust camouflage their presence. They are tricksters that change the minute they are discovered. They come in many forms which I will detail from my experience as an observer. There are so many talented actors that are screened from their own success by these subconscious self-defense mechanisms. There are things we do as actors that we transplant onto our characters, but they have nothing to do with character. These protections are the enemy of your own true light. This is another reason why nine out of ten actors in an audition look the same. They are all protecting themselves from making a mistake. These protective screens make us all look the same, not because we are safe, but because we're all screened from our true image by their presence.

You can put up a wall that makes you feel safe from invasions or violation, but a negative remains. No one can see you through that wall. Your true spirit is blocked. You are opaque; out of sight. Now, let's say you are more experienced and you don't stone yourself in. Instead, you put up a screen just to keep the bugs out. Your experience has taught you that you can't be destroyed anymore, but you just don't want those annoying insects of the industry to get to you. You know, actors who always get cast, the theatre company who never hires you, the call back you always get yet the job always eludes you, a producer who seems to look through you and not at you—insects, annoyances. A screen will keep you safe, but they will never clearly see who you are through that protection. The screen diffuses a clear view of you.

A student comes back from a call-back audition and says, "I was horrible but it doesn't make any difference because I was up against actor X. Actor X is the director's favorite actor. I don't even know why they called me in." This is a screen. The actor who blew the audition eliminated themselves. All they could focus on was the other actor. If they had been up against anyone else they would have been focused on the role rather than the other person. They were horrible because they placed a screen around themselves. They knew (or thought they knew) what the end result would be. They felt insecure, out-matched and less than actor X. The audition was not about the joy of their process, connecting with the character they were auditioning for, opening up and listening to what was actually happening that day or working out with a director they have long admired. It was about something self-made—a screen. Protecting themselves from an outcome they had predetermined. The screen of predetermination is what kept that actor safe and also what kept them from engaging imagination, creativity and accessing the freedom of their true potential.

You have one thing that makes you different from every other actor on the planet. That one thing is YOU. Hiding , protecting , allowing outside influences to affect YOU, is the only mistake you can make. When you protect yourself you may feel safe, but you are sacrificing the one thing, no matter how naturally talented you are, that will keep you from being noticed. You become filtered by your own devices. Discover them. Work to remove them. Fear has no place in the process. Conscious or unconscious, it is the single biggest block to imagination and creativity.

I also must tell you that it doesn't actually exist. Fear does not exist without us. We create it out of our negative experiences, inherit it from our parents, friends and colleagues. If we could harness all the energy we enlist to create our fears and turn it around to our advantage, we could accomplish things beyond our dreams. This is what makes a dynamic actor. No fear.

How do you get into a swimming pool? I'm assuming you can swim just like I'm assuming you can act. Do you start at the shallow end and painfully wet yourself ankle, to shin, to knee, to waist, fearing the cold water? You know full well that you are going to immerse your body anyhow! Do you just jump in? When you start to do laps after finally adjusting to the pool, are you worried you will drown?! You've been swimming all these years now; some of you since you were children. You are not going to drown. You may miss a stroke here and there, but you are not going to drown. So why fear what won't happen? A missed stroke or two in auditions just doesn't matter and will probably go unnoticed. It's all those people who are frightened to death of drowning that look alike.

You can swim. Trust that. Remove this panicked look from your face. Let you body relax. Trust yourself. Focus on your character. You're safe. Stop protecting yourself from something that can't happen. Use this anxiety to fuel your character rather than your unfounded insecurities. Use the audition process to practice removing your blocks, not to get a job.

Strip your protections. Start today. Come on in! The water's fine!

Inside Protection

This is the most common form of protection I have observed. The extreme case is obvious to discern. It looks or feels like the words of the script are printed on the inside of a person's eye sockets. The actor appears to be reading them and simultaneously interpreting the lines inside their own head. It's really safe in there. Just you and the script. In fact, the actor may be so engrossed in the reading that it precludes all other activity in the room. The actor is totally isolated by the words of the character. This actor very rarely, if ever, makes a mistake or drops a line. This actor may also have your lines indelibly painted in there, too. When you miss a line, the inside-protected actor will remind you of your mistake. It's all about getting the lines right, which, in my mind, is an assumed task. I assume you will get your lines right before we open. This is not the primary reason for rehearsals. If you are thinking of nothing else but the lines and blocking, you are inside-protected.

The inside protected actors I have known are extremely conscientious. I have one student in the class I'm currently teaching that serves as a prime example. Mike is ahead of himself. He is pushing hard to succeed at something he seems to have an affinity for—acting. He has taken two acting classes and never been in a play. He has been successful in the laboratory of the classroom. He has worked very hard and received a great deal of positive reinforcement from his teachers and classmates. He is passionately excited about his potential. He feels like he is starting to get it "right" and is highly motivated to continue this rapid progress he perceives. He comes to my class holding tightly to his newly learned techniques but they are all inside him. When he does his first monologue in front of a group of actors he believes are much more experienced he holds his past success with this monologue even closer. He wants to demonstrate his natural affinity for acting. He wants to "show" us and get it "right." He forgets a line and completely collapses and, for a moment, is broken. He apologizes to his classmates and me—twice. He digs in even deeper. All of his concentration is compressed inside his head. He wants more than anything to get through his monologue without forgetting a line. He begins again and moves mechanically, methodically emphasizing the same words repeating the exact same gestures we observed on his first attempt. Actually, they're not exactly the same but what we sense is that Mike is using all of his focus and energy to make them precise. It's all inside—inside protection.

Mike got through that monologue without a mistake and I know he returned to his seat completely satisfied. He had redeemed himself. He had accomplished a reenactment of what worked so well in his previous two classes. Unfortunately the only human connection he made was the sigh of relief he emitted after his second "more perfect" attempt was completed. It was genuine because it was not planned, protected, or anticipated. It was an accident and he revealed his truth not his character's.

Your inside protection may not be this exacerbated. It may take a more subtle form. In life, when you really want something from someone, let's say marriage. When you propose to the love of your life you extend yourself out to that person. You project what you want with all of your heart. You don't keep it buried inside of yourself anymore. It has probably been there for weeks, months, maybe even years. When the big day comes you liberate it from within extending it with your passion. You are no longer inside-protected on the subject of marriage. You have released your desire. The inside-protected actor holds not only the lines but the feelings, passions and needs of their character inside their eyes. The day of proposal never arrives. They experience everything but can't take the risk to release it or even communicate it to another actor onstage. Keeping it inside themselves enables them to feel safe. It is their protection but the drama never extends beyond this point, so it is empty, lifeless and disconnected from the imaginary world of the play as well as the other actors onstage. If you feel isolated and always get your lines right, you are probably inside-protected.

The Way Out

First of all you must begin to allow yourself the privilege of making mistakes. It's not easy. This is embossed in your life. Parents, teachers, supervisors and friends demand things that you have always worked to deliver as close to perfect as possible. Acting has nothing to do with demands others put on you. Acting only has to do with you. What you demand of yourself. Now, many will say, "I demand perfection." If that describes your reaction, know that you will have the greatest distance to travel. Perfection is irrelevant in art. Something can be a perfect work of art, but that has nothing to do with perfection. Your first steps must be toward a process focus. Forget about any results. Results are your enemy. Results, by definition, place your focus on the end of the journey instead of the road beneath your feet.

If you must be perfect, work on that at home. Study your lines. Make your connections. Find and dig for your character's moment of recognition. Think. Think. Think. Do you feel better? Now leave all that alone when you begin to rehearse. Trust that you have done the work. If it's valid it will reappear as a natural extension of what you're doing in today's work.

When you rehearse, focus, not on the things you know, as if to prove the fact that you have done your homework, but on the actual information that's coming into the rehearsal. Listen to your scene partner instead of subvocalizing your next line over in your mind. If you are doing a monologue, focus on the moment the character is composing what they are trying to clarify or articulate. The character doesn't know the exact words they are going to use. You do as the actor, but the character is making it up as they go along.

There is a story about the late great actor James Dean that speaks to this acting dilemma. James Dean only did three films but was extremely natural on camera. He had very little experience but created the illusion of a deep inner life for each character he portrayed. Many of his contemporaries, actors with many years of experience, would approach him with the same question: "How do you appear so natural? It seems as though you are making it up on the spot." His reply went something like this: "Well, I never really learn my lines completely so I'm always trying to recall what my character is supposed to say. I usually am in the process of making it up on the spot just like my character is."

Now this is an acceptable approach for a film actor because if he actually forgets his line and can't make up a better one on the spot you can always re-shoot the scene until you get precisely what works for the scene. This method of not completely learning your lines would only lead to chaos in the theatre in front of a live audience where you only have one chance to get what you want out of a scene, or the entire play for that matter. In the theatre you must approach the same problem from a completely different place. In the theatre you must know your lines so well that you *can't* forget them. Once you have accomplished this you can now employ the "Dean Method" and place your focus on creating the illusion that your *character* doesn't know what he is going to say and is trying to make it up on the spot.

You do the same thing every day of your life. You know what you want, but you never know exactly how or the precise words you will employ to articulate what you need. That's where your focus is in life—making it up as you experience the previous moment. That's the illusion you must create for each moment of the character on stage.

This is, in fact, the dichotomy of acting. It's totally false, meaning you know exactly how it's going to turn out, yet the character has to look like it's happening to them for the first time. Every time you run the same scene or monologue over and over, it must look like you're just making it up on the spot. That's where your focus needs to be directed. The first time, every time you run it. You don't have time to focus on getting your line right. It is actually the most useless piece of information in this moment of life you are creating on stage. Of course you must get the line right. I expect that as a minimum contribution. Learn your lines so you can actually rehearse the moment you are in.

You will forget many lines, transpose others and this is a good thing. Use your mistakes as a guide for what you need to study tomorrow. Study the lines you miss so you don't forget them in the next rehearsal when your focus is again fixed on the present tense actions and reactions of your character. Be your own judge. You know when you are subvocalizing your lines. Stop it. When you hear yourself and those voices in your head you know your focus is in the wrong place. Admit it to yourself. Force yourself to listen to what the other characters are saying to you onstage. When you listen intently you will forget some of your lines— that's good. What you need to practice at rehearsal is listening. Take the risk to extend your character's wants and needs out of your head and into the imaginary world of the play. That's why they call it a play! Come out and play!

If you're only struggling to remember your lines you begin to dread every word, which is exactly what you are feeling when you get a line wrong—dread. Yes, you must know your lines! . . . But you must know them so well that you forget about them.

Another Way Out Or How to Learn Your Lines

Don't memorize your lines. This approach is counterproductive. Give yourself the experiences of your character and remember the lines from the images of those experiences. Learn a character's thought process. Don't memorize words.

Every human being has a unique way of processing their thoughts and you must explore your character's ideology through their specific word choices. An actor came up to me the other day and wanted to know if they could transpose some words in a speech they were learning. When I inquired why they said they just couldn't remember them the way they were written. The phrasing seemed uncomfortable to them. "It's not something I would normally say," replied the actor. Because it is so difficult is the reason you must learn the phrase the exact way it is written. That is the difference between you and your character. *Their* specific way of speaking. It is your job to figure out the character's history and motivation for phrasing his speech in the specific manner. You must make a game or a story up that moves you closer to that character's life experience rather than changing the dialogue to fit with your experience as the actor.

Approach your lines as a creative learning experience as opposed to a task of memorization. Memorization is high school. "Memorize those facts, because there will be a pop quiz tomorrow." Sure, you memorized them. You got an A+ on your quiz, but what you "learned" was gone by the next day.

Building a character is about absorbed knowledge. You must create specific memories of your character's life and speak your lines from your creations. You may forget lines but you will always remember the images of the character's experience. The source of each word is invention based on accumulated experience. The line by itself is completely useless.

Here is a simplified example from a short play by David Mamet. Pick character A or B and see how quickly you can learn your lines.

B: I bet I know where you got that ice cream cone.

A: Where?

B: Down the mall.

A: That's right.

B: What did you pay for it?

A: Eighty-five cents.

B: Eighty-five cents . . .

A: That's right.

B: Is that with the tax?

A: No.

B: What is it with the tax?

A: Eighty-nine.

B: Eighty nine. That's right. I bought one there. (*pause*) I bought one there yesterday. What kind is it?

A: What kind is it?

B: Yes.

A: Butternut

B: Butternut. (*pause*) Mmmmmm. Unh.

If you picked character A in this sample scene, here is the experience you will give yourself. You went to the mall. You bought a butternut ice cream cone that cost eighty-five cents. There was four cents tax, so the total cost was eighty-nine cents. That's it entirely. Once you have that memory stored all you do is listen

and answer the questions you are asked. Why memorize the order of the lines when all you need is the information gotten from
your character's experience at the mall? This will allow you the
luxury to focus on the things that are actually important.

Character B is a little more complex because this character
is more active than reactive. You need to think of your information a little differently. If your character is interested in character
A, sexually, then "I bet I know where you got that ice cream
cone", and all the lines that follow are designed to attract and
make an impression. On the other hand, if you decide your character is not the least bit attracted to character A then, "I bet I
know where you got that ice cream cone", becomes idle chatter
from a person with nothing better to do than talk to strangers in
the park. All the lines that follow would be learned with that
specific intent in mind.

Try the following: you went to the mall yesterday. You bought
a cone that cost eighty-nine cents. You almost bought a butternut cone, but changed your mind at the last minute. You have an
attraction to character A and want to strike up a conversation.
Your objective is to try to make contact and to make a good impression. Combine your need with your experience yesterday
and you have learned all your lines without memorizing them.
You make a game out of your character's life and you play the
game. It's a creative adventure. It's fun. Learning your character
is no longer an assignment of memorization but play. Make your
character play and you will take the first big steps out of being
inside-protected. You are, in fact, forcing yourself into the
character's world by creating experiences you will remember as
opposed to memorized lines you will most certainly forget or have
to protect yourself to remember.

Be patient. Understand that making these adjustments will
take time. Make mistakes. Encourage the process by changing
your focus from lines to remembered experiences. Learn from
your mistakes. Take what you have learned back to rehearsal and
rededicate yourself to your newly refined experiences. Make mistakes

.. learn .. create .. Make mistakes ... Learn ... Create ... Keep playing this game and you will find the true path to your character along with eliminating your own voice from inside your head.

Outside Protection

The outside-protected actor literally judges what is good and what is ineffective while they are simultaneously performing their work. They are not really acting because the source of their involvement is located in a position of ineffective-ness-outside of themselves. By the time the outside-protected actor receives the information, it's too late to do anything about it. The outside protected actor listens and reports back to their creative center with messages of fear, praise, ambiguity and false security. You can no longer have control over what you have already spoken. Listening to yourself only aberrates every moment that could otherwise have a chance of succeeding. Every time you rise to workout your monologues you must let go of your technique, intellectual knowledge, text analysis and all the decisions you have previously made concerning your character. They are inside of you and, if they are relevant to the present tense moments your character is going through, they will appear. You can't force them! You can't be in two places at the same time; inside your character and outside observing.

I think this problem arises because actors have to work by themselves. They can go to a class or be coached only once or twice a week. The remainder of the time is spent working alone. As the actor works through their material they feel an obligation to judge it as well. They practice this repeatedly until splitting their energy becomes an instinctual action that is carried with them every time they work out their material.

Students often ask me how to practice between our class sessions. And I tell them that it is essential to know what you're working on while you are working. If you are developing ideas, enlarging on research or analyzing characters' motivations and needs that is a cognitive process. You have to think and act simultaneously. It's okay to step outside and take a look but you must be conscious of this fact. You are doing it for a reason. Once this work is done you must be able to practice letting it go. Your focus must change. You can't look for the result you have been seeking. You must now practice the process. You must completely focus on your character. You will never know the outcome of this work until you come to class. You have to practice complete immersion and trust yourself completely.

Great athletes do this constantly. They work out their problems on the practice field. They focus on their technique, analyze approach and break down the mechanics of their sport to examine every detail. The practice field is designed for this specific activity but in order to win the game they must trust their technique and move their focus directly to the target that registers a score. Nothing matters but that target. The actor's target is staying in the moment—being lost in that particular moment of their character's life.

You can never achieve a full performance by splitting your focus. You are not capable of evaluating any aspect of your process while you are engaged in the process itself. This is easy to understand intellectually, but nearly impossible to execute emotionally. Every lesson learned from our parents, teachers and society screams at us to get it right. It is in our cells. It is the most human of all instincts, and you must work every day towards focusing on the things you can control. The outside-protected actor is just afraid of doing something wrong so they listen to themselves to make sure everything is going right. Their protection is their block.

If you hear voices in your head and those voices all belong to you, then you are most likely outside-protected.

Seven Ways Out

1. Read "Stop Listening to Yourself." (Page 19)
2. Trust your homework.
3. Trust your good intentions.
4. Trust your instincts.
5. Trust your collaborators.
6. Trust your hard work and process.
7. If you can't find anything to trust, begin a search immediately.

Pacing Protection

Once I knew an actor who understood his character completely. His research was flawless. He could tell me why he was doing everything and his reasons could not be disputed. Every pause. Everything. I could ask him to repeat the monologue several times and each attempt was a template of the other. When I asked him to do it double time he tried but couldn't get through it without making a mistake, rather, what he perceived as a mistake. When I asked him to take more time such as making each pause twice as long as before he didn't know what to do with the extra time. He lost the entire focus of what his character was saying. He could only get through the monologue when I let him return to the pace at which he had learned it. He had rehearsed his homework into the monologue. His monologue was about his research rather than the character's needs. The pauses had to do with the actor not the character. The actor felt safe but the character never got a chance to speak. The character's monologue became the living proof of the actor's homework.

This protection has to do with rhythm; the pace at which you release your character's thoughts. Many artists believe that rhythm is the single biggest indicator of meaning. There is a whole school of acting developed by David Mamet and company that puts its focus on this single important element. It is essential that choices of rhythm be directly linked to the character. What happens when the actor is pacing-protected is that the rhythm of speech (especially monologues) is adjusted to a speed that the actor feels can safely maintain access to the correct line. The most common symptoms of this protected actor is a steady pace, a plodding pace or occasionally a race to the finish of the monologue.

What the pacing-protected actor can't do is change the pace of the monologue without forgetting lines. To me change is the essence of life. With each breath we inhale new elements. With each step we change the ground beneath our feet. The earth is rotating. The universe is expanding. Our lives are evolving every second and since we are the channel for the characters we play, our characters must evolve with us. As we repeat a monologue we learn something new. We change. The next time it is performed should reflect that growth. Rhythm must be based in the present tense. What is my character feeling today? Yes, I've built a beautiful frame for my character's life and I must stay within the boundaries of that frame but the picture of the character I paint today needs to be free and based in today's events.

The pacing-protected actor can never be in touch with their character using the device of rhythm. All decisions as to the pace are rooted in the actor's need to have a moment, a pause or no pause, that consistently trips the memory of the line. The pacing-protected actor, like the inside-protected actor, rarely forgets a line, but the character they are trying to become is totally diffused by this protective pacing screen. The pacing-protected actor learns only one way to say each line. Every pause is character developed and actor-filled. Each never-ending stream of words is completely disconnected from character, let alone any human connection.

This is fear-based. If I learn how to say it and how fast, then I can memorize that and get it right every time. Getting it right for this actor means getting through the entire monologue without a mistake. In trying to set its correctness you are doing the one thing that will always keep it from being effective. You are centered in fear, and nothing creative or inspired can be born in that atmosphere. Two seconds of inspiration or a real human connection is far more impressive than two minutes of perfect line readings.

The Way Out

L earn the lines so well that the lines are not the issue. Don't work on your lines with any interpretation involved even though you may believe in only one meaning or character intent. If your singular approach is really valid it will always be present. Engraving it into the line learning process will only make it overly emphasized or redundant. Trust your understanding of the character and situation of the play. You can't learn or memorize a moment, because that moment is never going to be exactly the same. You are using all your energy to do the one thing you can't do—be exactly the same every time. Even if you could accomplish exact repetition it would be false and disconnected from the evolving action of a live performance. Try one or all of the following suggestions:

Re-read "How to Learn Your Lines." (Page 33)

Practice your lines at different paces

· Speed Run
· Sing the lines
· To a jazz beat
· To a Rock and Roll beat
· To a classical beat
· Speed run each individual line (pause), then the next line (longer pause) next line (shorter pause).
· Do your lines with a completely different impulse
· As an auctioneer
· As a drill sergeant
· As an F.M. radio jock

My favorite exercise involves making up a list of questions that the lines in your monologue are the answer to. I do a variation of this exercise frequently in class especially when I work with students who are interpreting rather than connecting with their character's lines. It's the same process only I make up the questions and ask them directly to the student instead of writing them on cards. I want the student to focus only on answering the questions. I want a direct response to the question—nothing more. The results are always immediate and positive. The student is responding to a direct stimulus in an honest manner. Most students enjoy doing scene work over monologues because they have another person to interact with. It doesn't seem like a mountain of words that only they are responsible for. Creating these questions makes your monologue a direct interaction like a scene between two characters. You begin to focus your response to each element of the monologue in a direct rather than an interpretive manner. This directness will now permeate the core of your monologue.

Now, put each question on flash cards then flip them over one by one and answer the questions with the exact line in your monologue.

Below is Petruchio's monologue from *Taming of the Shrew* Act IV, Scene i. It looks like a giant mountain to climb:

Thus have I politically begun my reign,
And 'tis my hope to end successfully,
My falcon now is sharp and passing empty,
And till she stoop she must not be full gorged,
For then she never looks upon her lure.
Another way I have to man my haggard,
To make her come and know her keeper's call,
That is, to watch her as we watch these kites
That bate and beat and will not be obedient.
She eat no meat today, nor none shall she eat.
Last night she slept not, nor tonight she shall not.
As with the meat, some undeserved fault

I'll find about the making of the bed,
And here I'll fling the pillow, there the bolster,
This way the coverlet, another way the sheets.
Ay, and amid this hurly I intend
That all is done in reverent care of her,
And in conclusion she shall watch all night.
And if she chance to nod I'll rail and brawl
And with the clamour keep her still awake.
This is a way to kill a wife with kindness,
And thus I'll curb her mad and headstrong humor.
He who knows better how to tame a shrew,
Now let him speak—'tis charity to show.

Here is a list of potential questions with answers taken directly from the text.

Q: What have you just done?

A: Thus have I politicly begun my reign,

Q: How do you think it will turn out?

A: 'tis my hope to end successfully.

Q: How is your calculated plan succeeding so far?

A: My falcon now is sharp and passing empty, and till she stoop she must not be full gorged, for then she never looks upon her lure.

Q: What other methods might you employ to tame her?

A: Another way I have to man my haggard to make her come and know her keeper's call, that is, to watch her as we watch these kites that bate and beat and will not be obedient.

Q: What happened today?

A: She eat no meat today, nor none shall she eat.

Q: What happened last night?

A: Last night she slept not, nor tonight she shall not.

Q: What will you devise to keep her awake?

A: As with the meat, some undeserved fault I'll find about the making of the bed.

Q: What will you do when you find these bed flaws?

A: Here I'll fling the pillow, there the bolster, this way the coverlet, another way the sheets.

Q: Don't you think this treatment is a little extreme?

A: Ay, and amid this hurly I intend that all is done in reverent care of her.

Q: Sum up your approach for me.

A: And in conclusion she shall watch all night and if she chance to nod I'll rail and brawl and with the clamour keep her still awake.

Q: Why go to all these lengths?

A: This is a way to kill a wife with kindness, and thus I'll curb her mad and headstrong humor.

Q: Do you think your methods will actually work?

A: He who knows better how to tame a shrew, now let him speak—

Q: (pause)

A: Tis charity to show.

Put some creativity into methods of learning your lines. Have fun creating the questions that your dialogue answers. Now, when you play this game focus on actually answering the questions. This way you will be rehearsing a directness into the core of your monologue.

If you really want to see how well you know your monologue shuffle your cards and see if you can do them out of sequence. Also, don't feel locked in to your original questions—things change, let your questions evolve with your specific understanding of the monologue. There are no rules! Be creative!

Movement Protection

This manifests itself in your process in several ways. During a monologue the movement-protected actor will often wander aimlessly about the stage. There is no recognizable motivation attached to this movement. It is movement or activity for protection sake; this actor will focus stage right, then stage left and back again. They rarely take their focus straight out where the casting director or director are seated. As long as this actor is in motion there is safety in the ever-changing focus that motion creates.

They are externalizing their internal uneasiness. Most movement-protected actors are unaware of these excessive evasions. Their movement is their lifeline. It seems active. They feel engaged in a character-motivated action that is vital and endemic to the monologue. "No. I'm not nervous. My character is working out their dilemma. I'm pacing in thought," can often be the defensive reply when I point this out. I can accept that, but the actor's constant movement only demonstrates what's going on in that character's mind. It's an outward show of confusion that diffuses my attention. I can't really focus on the internal effect of this dilemma unless you stop moving and let me in or make specific rather than random choices of when to pace. When you can internalize the action of a human being actively searching for a solution, you will draw my attention towards you. If you are constantly moving you are using that movement as your own protection.

Excessive movement doesn't always involve wandering aimlessly about the stage. Actress Anne who is in my current class came into class last evening with Portia's monologue from *Julius Caesar*. She thoroughly understood the text as well as Portia's special relationship with Brutus. A true partnership. A relationship ahead of its time. Anne captured Portia's confusion perfectly but embodied her monologue with these very large stylistic gestures. Her movement was constant. There were broad gestures that seemed to encompass the universe. She was also extending her arms towards her husband an inordinate number of times. The activity of working through Portia's present tense dilemma with Brutus for some reason didn't seem active enough so Anne began to move and her actions took my eye away from Portia's internal struggle. The gestures Anne unconsciously chose were instinctively correct. The broad gestures made the statement of the larger stakes—the betrayal of trust that encompasses their entire relationship. The extension of her arms outward was Portia reaching out to Brutus—imploring him to confess the dark secrets Portia knows he holds within. Her gestures, however, divert my focus and force me to take in the entire room. They diffuse my point of contact with the character, and prevent me from being drawn into Portia's world.

The movement-protected actor understands the central issues of their character. They are working hard to resolve them, and that hard work is the only thing that is being demonstrated. The character's internal conflict can't be observed through the blur of the moment. If, when you are working on your character, you are in constant motion, try internalizing that desire to move. Your instinctual feeling of unrest is probably correct. That is what your desire to move is saying to you. Find a way to transplant that restless energy inward. Move only when motivated by a direct character action such as; I must or need to face the protagonist directly, or I need a drink, or I must sit down. Your character should need to take a movement-related action. It takes energy to move externally and often there are direct payoffs of that external expenditure. Be certain that each movement has its origin in your character's needs and objectives. Use your instinctual desire to move as an indicator of what you can make happen internally. Turn your protection into a barometer and use these informative instincts to their full advantage.

Another symptom of the movement-protected actor is no movement. A transfixed stare creates a pocket of safety for this actor. They find some spot on the wall and freeze their focus. The entire monologue is delivered to this fixed location. Once again it is either three quarters to the left of center or three quarters to the right, but rarely directly over the auditor's head. I have been teaching *Acting by Mistake* for almost seven years and about ten percent of the actors I have worked with hold on to this deeply fear-based protection with all their might. Actor Jerry in 1994 told me that if he saw anything else but that spot he couldn't remember his next line. Actress Elaine in 1996 said that her audition coach taught her this technique to help her black out all distractions not unlike the black hole that the bright stage lights create for the actor in a production. Actor Jeff last year told me that he just didn't know where else to look.

During a scene the spot-fixed actor does a similar thing to the other actors on stage. They become spot-fixed, not in the other actor's eyes, but frequently just above or below. They can't make direct contact, because it is the avoidance of that contact that keeps them safe. If they look directly into the eyes, the line is forgotten because a new element is immediately introduced— another human being's existence.

Observe conversations in life. Observe your own conversations. You don't stare at the object of your conversation every second and you shouldn't do it on stage. It's unnatural.

In auditions finding an imaginary spot where the person you are speaking to is located is important. When an actor can create the feeling that someone else is in the room it enhances the reality of their monologue. Once you locate that spot use it but don't abuse it. Relate to it rather than giving it your full concentration.

You feel safer with a tight spot focus because you are less likely to catch distractions. Don't be afraid of distractions. If distractions are part of what is actually happening in that room, trust your character to work through them. Don't divide yourself into the actor who is distracted and the character who can't react to the distraction.

Trust yourself and your knowledge of the monologue to take in what is actually happening. If your character's world extends to the audience then you must make adjustments to their behavior. I have, on occasion, when asked a rhetorical question by an auditioner during their monologue, improvised an answer. I purposely supplied a reaction the actor did not expect. Some actors are taken aback almost as if I had violated some unspoken rule. They pause, as the actor, then return to their well-rehearsed routine. Others are delighted by my response and will play with this surprise information. Still others are confused. Should I react? Shouldn't I? What is he doing? If your character is talking to the audience you should expect them to talk back. If you don't you're probably not really talking to them in the first place. When your character's action is to talk to the audience then use distractions in the room to your character's advantage.

If your character is talking to an imaginary character you have placed in the room the distractions are outside of your area of concentration. Your character should ignore them. No matter what the situation the character must believe in their world. Once you begin your audition all decisions are character-based. Only the actor can be distracted. Use your character's mask to hide behind any distractions. On one occasion in a large group audition, commonly known as a "cattle call" the power went out in the theatre. The actor auditioning at the time was only two lines away from the conclusion of his monologue when the blackout came. He paused momentarily (everyone in the room did as well), there was a silence and out of the blackness we heard, "I know you can't see me Muriel but I want you to know I still love you." It got a tremendous laugh and when the lights were restored five minutes later the actor went to the stage again to state his name. He received a healthy applause and I'm sure several call backs. He used the unexpected distraction.

Spot fixing is like putting blinders on a race-horse. At the track they are used for horses who panic, seeing or sensing other horses on the either side of them. It invades their focus and consequently they lose their stride. Blinders force their concentration toward the finish line ahead. Don't put blinders on. Get involved in the race. The race is what's happening. The finish line is the last thing you should be concerned with. Process is the actors' focus. Be challenged by current events. Be in the room. Don't hide or run to the safety and protection of an arbitrary spot.

I have even observed actors introducing their monologues to this imaginary spot. This is fear-based and the director as well as the casting director will pick up this fear before you even begin your monologues. Use your audition to actually talk to your auditors. Make eye contact with them. Shake their hand if they extend it. Use your entrance as an opportunity to play another character—you. Be yourself. Connect to what is happening in the present tense and your audition will have a spontaneous energy. These are the things you need to work on in your audition process. Go to an audition to work instead of focusing on getting the job. Connect with the process. The job is the finish line. Keep your eyes off it. That spot may keep you safe but it's a false sense of security that will in no way benefit your audition.

Use rehearsals and time with an acting coach to work through these blocks. Rehearsals are there to workshop your weaknesses. Enter each rehearsal to challenge your skills and do the things you've never done before. Many actors say, "I wish I could try this, or . . . I wish I had the ability to really listen to what is being said . . ." You have these capabilities—you just need practice to bring them forward.

Spend an entire rehearsal just listening to what everyone is saying. Keep your focus on the information coming to your character from the other actors, the director, and even the props.

Actually taste that cup of tea when you are served. If someone brought you a desired refreshment right now you would taste it. It might motivate you to say something back. It might be so delicious you just savor it for a moment but it would be information you would take in. If you do this you will most likely miss many cue pick-ups and make mistakes with your actual lines. These mistakes should be what you study. These are the guides to the true development of your character. Rehearsals are for practicing courage. You will achieve a courageous performance only when you challenge yourself and your skills each time you work out.

Rehearsals should be a laboratory for creativity, not a practice field of repetition. Discover what you need to change and use rehearsals to conquer these specific obstacles. Don't avoid your own success. Remove your blocks and protections one at a time. Confront your fears; you created these specters and you can dissolve them.

Performance Protection

This is for actors who love a finished product. They find great solace in the final result they have achieved though their hard work. They rely on accomplishment and hide behind its bravura each time they perform. It's all about performance. The word discovery has been eliminated from consideration. When you attempt to change any aspect of their sealed-in performance, big problems ensue. This actor is often histrionic, self-contained, self-involved and safe within the formula of success they have created. Growth has ceased. Performance has ensued and all negotiation with change has become impossible. The actor may perform quite brilliantly but the brilliance has limitation attached to it now. If it's audition material, this actor has put it in a 'can' visible to all perceptive enough to see though the protection of performance. If it's a production you have gotten the best performance out of this actor on opening night. If you're on stage with this person, expect exactly the same event each night.

Performance protected actors are rarely aware of their well rehearsed creative block. You're not going to be able to change them because change is what the protected actor fears most. If something is different it throws them off their pre-destined track so abruptly that they forget their lines. You can give them the exact same cue line, place it in a slightly different package and they will go blank. If you tell other actors how to deliver lines, if you tell other actors they missed a blocked move and if everything must go exactly right every time you're on stage you are most likely performance-protected.

It's a natural human instinct to desire completion. We begin, so therefore there is a conclusion, a point at which you say, "My work is done." This is true in acting but the work is not completed on stage until the final curtain falls. An audition monologue never stops evolving until you have used it for the last time. Growth must continue because it is the natural order of life. Is there anything that is exactly the same each day? Are you precisely the same each morning you awake? Things change. The actors' art form is the evolution and reaction to these differences. Truly great actors revel in these variations because change is infused by the life force. Even with death there is a constant change called decay. I understand the urge to finish but in acting you must be patient and live through the entire event. Trust the work you have done each day so intently that you can open your vision, come out of your protected performance and join what is changing right now.

One of the best pieces of advice I ever heard came from a director friend of mine, Ken Marini. Ken was a guest in my audition class and, as a practicum for my students, they presented two audition monologues for his comments. I also watched because it is an education for me to watch my students respond outside of the safe, supportive classroom environment I try to create. Ken said. "When you walk into an audition think of it as going to a first rehearsal. You are open, willing to meet all the people you will be working with. Ready to begin a process; ready to begin a collaboration. Instead of going into an audition and introducing your monologues by saying, "I will be performing two pieces today." Start by saying "I'm working on these two monologues," or even, "I'd like to show you these two pieces I've been working on." Now, there is a person I want to work with, someone who is working, refining all the time. This actor is open to negotiation and collaboration. Someone who doesn't want to perform for me but prefers to roll up his or her sleeves and says, "Here's what I've been working on. What do you think?"

Think of this approach in your own terms. Don't you feel comfortable, excited and curious going to a first rehearsal? Compare that with the feeling of an audition. Which is more relaxed? Which is more creative? Which defines who you really are and what you really want out of the entire process? When you try to achieve a finished product you are always focused on the wrong event. You are focused on something you can't control— the result. Enjoy your hard work. Trust those results. Get involved in the creative process and the finished product will be the result of your passions and desires. Step outside of the finished product you've been hiding behind and see what's out there. Make adjustments. Challenge yourself to create beyond your present limitations.

The Way Out

Spend all your rehearsal time listening, looking, feeling and seeing everyone and everything that surrounds your character. Don't' punish yourself for mistakes. Instead, be encouraged and motivated by them. Base everything you say as the character on the present tense moments in rehearsal. Get out of your head and connect with your heart. It is your guide for dealing with change. It is expanding or contracting every moment of your existence. Feel and trust that. Leave your homework at home and come ready to give any or all of it up.

If you're working on a monologue, do it differently. Do it as if:
- You're talking to a child
- You're talking to a dog
- You're talking to a stranger
- You're talking to your best friend
- You're giving a speech
- You're talking to yourself
- Use your own imagination and take this simple exercise any direction you desire. Try to feel, *not listen* to which of these focus changes is most applicable to your character.
- Compose the words of your monologue as you go through it. You, the actor knows the words of the monologue so forget them. Take them out of your focus and re-direct it to composition of thought your character is involved in.
- Go to different locations, i.e. bathroom, basement, study, living room, kitchen, park, etc. try to use your senses to absorb

the environment. React to this new information and see where it leads you.

· Whatever you do, do not listen to yourself or monitor the results in any way. Trust your instincts and feelings.

All of the above suggestions are opportunities to take your rigid "performance" out of one single context. I have a beautiful golden retriever named Ahne. When I teach in my home she is always a tremendous help. Ahne will just sit there and listen to anyone quietly, attentively. When my students focus on her faithful eyes it brings something out in them. Their monologue is always affected by Ahne's presence. If I give my student a piece of popcorn (Ahne lives and breathes for popcorn. Her entire being becomes animated.) my student now has control over the dog. No longer is Ahne passively listening but instead is actively engaged. Once again the monologue changes. The change is directly related to the circumstances of that special interaction—that chemistry between Ahne and my student. As students rehearse their monologue the repetition chokes the spontaneity out of the encounter they are having with that invisible other person. You tend to remember what "works" more than the elements that make each day unique. The performance protected actor needs to trust their past successes completely and let the present tense conditions penetrate the 'practiced' walls of performance. The above exercises will enable you to react to different stimuli and challenge your true understanding of character and present tense conditions. Just enjoy the journey. That's actually what will bring the spontaneity back to your work.

Decisions

On the first night of most classes I teach, I do an exercise I have developed over the years. It doesn't have a name, but here's the way it proceeds. If I have fifteen students I divide them into five groups of three. It is also important to note that the exercise is most effective when the participants don't know each other well. I tell each group that I want them to write a short scene that has a beginning, middle as well as a distinct ending. I also want this scene to make a point. Now the point doesn't have to be Shavian in nature. It should be simple. For example: Two people enter a bar (the third actor becomes bartender). They both start to drink. One chugs while the other sips. The bartender won't serve the guzzler anymore so they depart. The heavy drinker insists on driving. They both get into a car and the scene concludes with a collision of some sort. The point is obviously don't drink and drive. Next, I tell them they can't use or speak words when performing the scene. The actions should be so clear that actual dialogue is unnecessary. Pantomime the action and words. If you must make audible sounds, only gibberish can be employed. The final requirement of the exercise is that you can't use words to communicate with each other while you are writing the scene. An uncomfortable silence usually follows this instruction. I go on to say that you can't use paper, pencil, or pen to inscribe any ideas or dialogue either. Now it's really quiet . . . Any questions? Hands inevitably spring up. "How do we communicate our ideas?"

"You will have to figure that out by yourselves," I answer calmly.

"How long should it be?"

"I'm giving you fifteen minutes to write, direct and rehearse your scene. Don't worry about a time limit. Just make sure it has a beginning, middle, end and makes a point."

"How do we do that without speaking?"

"I don't know how you will do it, but I can tell you I've never seen any one fail in ten years of doing this exercise." Another pause. "You are going to want to cheat, it is only natural. You have been verbally communicating all you life. Don't succumb to these temptations. If someone in your group unconsciously or consciously begins to speak or write something down, just turn away from them until they stop. Trust the exercise! If you break the guidelines you only dilute the effect of the exercise. Any more questions?"

I try to separate each group. It's easy because it's a silent exercise, so I can place groups in hallways and stairwells. It's most effective if one group cannot observe another group's progress. I give them fifteen minutes and pass silently among them to observe their process. I give them a five-minute warning and when that time has passed, I call them all into the classroom to present their creations.

All the groups succeed to some degree, but the effectiveness of the scene is not the point of this exercise. Now, I let them talk. Everyone usually bursts into conversation. I let the conversation flow for a minute or two before I go around the room and ask the same question to each group: "Can you please describe your rehearsal process?" The explanations are remarkably similar. One person in the group got up and started doing a simple action. Another person observed what was going on and joined in. Finally, the third member enters, extending the ideas presented. Sometimes, one person initiates an idea no one understands. Yet another group member gets a new idea form this confusion and begins an activity that everyone is clearly motivated by. The scene is then developed from that point. Occasionally a participating student will have an entirely different understanding of their role than everyone else in the group. Anything can happen and usually does. The point of the exercise is not to create a completely realistic scene that makes perfect sense. After describing their rehearsals, I ask them to discuss what single event linked each group creation together.

Somebody started to do something. Someone made a decision. If no one made decision you would all be out in the hall staring at each other right now. If you never made a decision you could stay there the rest of your lives! Think about it! Decisions make things happen. In order to make something happen for yourself as an artist, you must make a decision. It might be wrong. It might be embarrassing but something will happen and you can proceed from that point. That is the whole point of making a decision in the first place; a point of origin. Right or wrong it launches the creative process.

In life, if you make no decisions, not much will happen to you. Many people live their entire life afraid to make decisions because they might be the wrong ones. A wrong decision is a blessing. It guides me to a better one. Having the courage to decide is the benchmark of a true artist.

Many actors walk into their first rehearsal and wait to be directed. They read the play, they do their research, but they make no decisions, fearing their instincts could be misguided. They wait to hear what the director thinks. They begin to surrender their power in the rehearsal process from day one.

Theatre is the actor's medium. The director won't be getting up on the stage opening night to guide your decisions. The actor has the power on stage. That power is born in the decision-making process. Collaborate with your director. Listen to everything they say. Let those ideas season the decisions you make about your character, but make your own decisions. Take the risk to be wrong or half right or completely right. It makes no difference what the results of your decisions are, but you must be involved in the process of making them. If your decision doesn't completely agree with the director, discuss the difference. This will clarify your role as a collaborator. Directors often bully actors. It can be quite intimidating, but you must contribute your ideas and inject your instincts into your character.

When casting a show, I like an actor who creates something about a character I never thought of. I like to work with a proactive artist who makes decisions. I don't have all the right answers. I'm desperately trying to ask the right questions. Everyone is unique. No one person should be the creator in theatre. Decide. Make yourself part of the process. Embrace the mistakes your bad decisions lead you to. Turn those mistakes into your own creations. Listen to what is going on around you. Make decisions based on that evolving input. Do your homework—make decisions. Come to rehearsal—make decisions based on what is happening that day; that moment. Listen to your director—make decisions. Make things happen for yourself by taking the risk to make a decision.

One Final Note

When I do the decision exercise some groups finish creating their scenes before the full fifteen-minute rehearsal time has elapsed. They think the exercise is complete and proceed back towards the classroom. I always intercept them and send them back into rehearsal. I ask them to continue adding details to their scene in the remaining time. Every moment can be utilized to make more decisions that will impact the depth and color of your work. Don't stop. Use all your time—not only with this exercise, but every other creative endeavor.

Surviving

You must be patient. You must wait for opportunities that will present themselves. You must trust yourself. You must work on all the things you have control over. You must believe in your good intentions and attend to them everyday. You must never give up or lose faith in your passions and you will survive.

Isn't there a story about a man in, I don't know, Arkansas? He worked his gold mine. He dug deeper every day for twenty-five years. He sharpened his tools. He believed in his imminent discovery. One day he sold his dream to a low bidder. He took the money and rested. One week and eighteen inches of stone later the low bidder struck gold. After twenty-five years and thousands of feet of rock, he rested eighteen inches from his vision.

I know both of these people. I know the low bidder. I see him every day, every day of my life. Everything falls into this one's lap. He is the blessed one. He gets cast in a showcase that I turned down. Steven Spielberg shows up to a performance, sees him in this god-awful play and casts him as the lead in his next film. I know the twenty-five year prospector intimately, and I'm not going to make the same mistake he did.

Surviving bad actors, rude directors, visionless producers, intolerable agents or completely passionless casting directors is the same story. They are the rocks you must move out of your path. Give them anything but what's truly inside you. Keep that inner actor for yourself. They wouldn't know what to do with it anyway. Hold on and you will survive.

The mark of a truly accomplished actor is surviving a bad director. The collaborative nature of our art form demands you to take a negative and turn it around to your advantage. Negatives will always be present. You must learn to revel in them. Dig yourself into your creative center and play with these devils. They are there to test the true artist inside you. If they didn't reveal critical issues they wouldn't frustrate, anger and totally confuse you. You can let your feelings block you or you can use them for inspiration. It's your choice, but realize the stakes involved with each confrontation. The stakes are your tenacity, trust, passions and desires.

There will always be people to test you. Take the test. Learn from the results. Don't force the result you desire. Create your visions from the results of your best efforts. When the next test comes along, and it won't be long until it does, follow the same procedure. Best efforts plus observed results equals the creation of new ideology from your observations. Increase your power with each new project, audition or interview. Develop strength, confidence and wisdom based on your experience.

Doing it for yourself should be the premise of your creative choices. There are always people who will say, "Do this. Don't do that. It won't get you anywhere . . ." or, "How can you turn that down?! . . . You must take that offer. You may never have an opportunity like this again." I believe we all know deep inside what we want. I believe events occur that are sent to guide us in the direction of our creative path. I believe we have little voices inside us that we hear and ignore or are so busy "thinking" what's best for us that those little voices are never distinguished through the din of our cognitive process.

I read a book called *The Artist's Way* by Julia Cameron. That book brought me to the page everyday which led me right here. I write everyday. It releases the weight of my "thinking" from my developing artist's soul. Others meditate, run, do yoga, tai chi—

the list of choices is endless, but one thing remains constant; you must take care of yourself. You must desire change in order to survive. And you must do things that heighten your senses and allow you to trust and access the voices within. This is not new information but, for me, it has been a revelation. If you start today your revelation will come too.

It will be most difficult in the beginning. It will be frustrating as your process matures. Satisfaction will come if you keep digging, and when you reach the buried treasure that is your true process, you will look back and realize you have survived.

Follow Through

Everything natural in life seems to follow through. The seasons, the earth's rotation, the movement of the galaxies, the expansion of the universe and even my golf swing. Once an action is born, it creates a momentum unto itself that continues with its creator, changing as it moves along, forever embodied by its first instinct of birth.

I have observed thousands of monologues and scenes in my career. The ones I remember most have this same universal energy of follow through attached to them. Trusting where you are is the key ingredient of follow through. If what I am doing in the present moment is connected, that connection, if I trust myself enough, will guide me most naturally to my next connected moment and so on. It's like a long row of dominoes.. They fall, moment by moment, from the previous moment that was knocked over before. A force of follow through connects them.

For me, a laugh is the most natural form of human follow through. I believe laughter is life's most satisfying feeling. It supercedes sex because laughter has, at least for me, interrupted a sexual experience on more than one occasion. I can't recall one time when I have interrupted laughter to have sex. Maybe afterwards, but never in the middle of a good hard laugh. I can't stop the follow through of a laugh. It's too powerful. It's ingrained in every cell of my body. I trust it because it feels good. It stops time. It's taking me someplace I'm glad to be going. I am, in fact, like no other time in my life, totally enjoying the journey. There is such ease and relaxation to laughter. A good monologue or scene should feel the same way. A natural flow of energy that can't be stopped, suppressed or intellectualized. It's devoid of tension and pressure. It's all encompassing. It's a joy. It's own momentum keeps perpetuating itself.

Many actors confuse momentum with speed, but it's not the same thing. Speed is just fast. No particular reason, just fast; as in-do the exercise faster. Momentum has to do with an organic feeling that passes through your body. You can pause all you wish, as long as your pause is embodied by your momentum. A pause is a glorious gift rather than a resting place, and certainly not a place to stop. A pause is an opportunity to fill what you're doing with life. A place with no line responsibility. A place to revel, heighten or temper the moment before or the moment to come. When you are following them through, your pause should integrate the moment before. Hang on to that energy and use that to leap to your next word.

I can think of only one exception. When your character purposely halts their present tense moment in the action of the play to re-focus their energy towards a new beat or objective. Even then, your character still vibrates from the energy that precedes this new line of action. You can try to wipe yourself clear, but you can rarely accomplish it.

Think of your own experience. Let's say, for example, you're waiting at the airport for your lover to arrive. Over the PA system comes an announcement that the flight is delayed. You were expecting the person you love most in your life to walk though that gate in five minutes, but that just changed. Isn't the anticipation you were feeling wrapped up in the present moment? A brief fear may overcome you that the plane may have crashed. You stop yourself. You literally stop your energy and say, "Wait a minute. Everything is fine. Get a hold of yourself. Settle." You have stopped your momentum to say it will be fine, but those previous moments of anticipation are all tied up in this halting, this momentary tragic beat change. You can't think away natural emotional flow.

Another example. You're having the best game of your life in whatever field of play you may excel in. You are one moment away from a breakthrough victory, and you begin to get nervous anticipating the glorious result. You stop yourself. You say, "Just one more moment and I will achieve my personal best." Even though your entire body is working to center your focus for the final thrust to achievement, that flash of nerves you previously experienced is intrinsically tied into the present. You can't stop your natural emotional follow through.

One final example in the other extreme. Nothing is going well this day. It seems your career is truly stagnant. The pond of opportunity is so still that you can feel algae growing in the cracks of your artist soul. The phone rings. It's the opportunity you've been waiting for your entire career—out of the blue. Your life is forever changed by this extraordinary news. You accept. You hang up, sitting there in disbelief. That disbelief is what ties your previous depression to your present elation. You just can't escape this follow through. It's omnipresent and happening to you this very moment.

When you rehearse a monologue or a scene, this is what you should be exploring. The natural follow through of your character's life events. So often, I observe actors stop and begin anew. They take a scripted pause and come out of it in a completely unrelated direction. It is often disconnected from the moment, before the pause. When this happens, the actor is usually intellectualizing the character's new direction, based on some homework decision from the previous evening. What the actor is focusing on is the repetition of the intellectualized moment instead of the actual moment of follow through in their character's life.

Do that homework, but when you work, think of your work as a laugh. Once the laughter begins, trust the momentum of the moment to guide you naturally to the next and so on. Actors over-think out of fear. They are trying to get it right. You can't, so don't spend your energy trying. What you can consistently get right, is trusting what is actually happening to lead you to today's truth. Follow through. Trust yourself and all the work you have put into your character up to this point. Make mistakes. Make adjustments. Now go back with even greater trust to the actual flow of the character's life. The proof of the work lies in the freedom of the moment.

In rehearsal and performance, get involved with *now*. Follow through on now just as you are doing now.

Don't Explain. Don't Interpret . . . Just Tell It.

I get annoyed when writers, especially playwrights, *explain* their writing by putting the really *critical* words in *italics*. *These* are the words that *should* be emphasized. What bothers me is that *they* think I'm not bright enough to figure out what they mean without these *special* notations. It's like they are talking down to me on the page. Actors do this, too. Actually, they do it more often than not, which is why actors can look so different, yet still sound alike. They *explain* their dialogue. It's probably the most subtle form of indication, and its effect can be off-putting, to say the least.

Imagine if *I* tried to *teach* a class *explaining* almost *everything* I *said*. You would not last long in that class, believe me. You would feel like I was talking down to you; that *I* knew *everything* and *you* weren't bright enough to understand *anything* unless I *explained* it to you.

I think it is a natural instinct to want to explain yourself so when we have dialogue thrust in front of us we want to explain that, too. Actors seem to feel a need to interpret what the character is experiencing. They want the audience to understand and consequently explain their actions to enhance the audience's understanding of their character. The audience must be given the opportunity to create its own understanding of your character. That's what engages them in the play. They need to believe that you've had the experience rather than have that experience interpreted to them. It challenges their imagination and draws them closer to you. It's a mystery that's unfolding in front of them.

It's not unlike when you learn something. Knowledge can be a powerful thing. Many people after learning something new want to tell everyone about it. They are sharing the excitement of their new found gifts. They explain what they have learned to everyone. Others, having learned the same thing, will keep it to themselves and use this new information to empower their own actions. These actions will change their behavior and everyone will sense a change in this person, too. But the change will be more mysterious. "Why is he acting that way? What's going on? Something's different." Now they are engaged by your knowledge. You become an enigma.

Here's one more example. You all have actor friends. Everyone goes to auditions and is in a constant process of searching out opportunities. Some of your friends explain to you everything they are doing, how often they do it and what everyone else said about them. They constantly talk about all their possibilities at great length. All they do is talk about it but rarely do they do a good job. Then there is this friend who seems to work all the time but you never know exactly how they accomplish this . . . Who would you rather spend two hours with?

The actual dialogue of the play is the explanation. When an actor attempts to explain or interpret the explanation it becomes redundant; just like the actor who points to themselves each time they speak the pronoun "I" or points to you when referring to the only other character on stage.

Just tell it. Relate the character's experience to the written dialogue, so a point of view can emerge from the author's explanation of events. Don't serve it up to the audience. Package the author's events with the character's experience and tell it from that specific point of view. Your character was actually there. It needs no further explanation. You were there! Tell us what you experienced. Just tell it.

This will also prevent you from repeating your dialogue the

same way each run through. When you explain something, you tend to emphasize the same words each time because that is the clearest explanation. If you tell a story to a friend it will come out based on how you remember that experience and what you want that friend to know about it. If, later in the day, you see that same friend, and they ask you to repeat your story, it will not come out the exact same way. You tell it differently because you remember the experience and see it differently each time you tell it. Focus on remembering the event and simply tell what your character remembers. Don't explain. Don't interpret. Just tell me.

Trust

Trust is the antidote for fear. It is easily understood, but difficult to put into practice. I know of only one way to trust myself, and that is to do the work completely, religiously and faithfully each day. Consistency is the key that unlocks this personal confidence.

It's like studying for a final exam. If I cram the night before the test I can't trust my knowledge. Frequently, I can get away with a satisfactory result, but I am never relaxed. Trust requires a comfort level. If I don't study, even though I've been to class every day, I'm a basket case when the test is passed out. I'm deflated because of my lack of discipline. The only way to walk into that final was after doing the homework every day. Go to class, come home, do the exercises and synthesize the material into a greater understanding of the whole; learn it! When I learned it I could work with it. My knowledge was practical and portable.

It took me a long time to find something I truly loved to do in life. I'm familiar, all too familiar, with the cramming process. It dictated my approach to education for years because I was doing it for the wrong reasons. I was going to school for one reason, actually—to satisfy my parents. I studied very little. I learned even less until one day I discovered something that brought it all together for me—theatre. I clearly found my passion in life and the learning process finally began during my junior year of college. I worked hard every day and enjoyed the process. My grade point average went from 2.6 to 3.8 to 4.0 not because I had to but because I loved what I was doing. Trust and love of the game are inextricably tied to each other. If you are cramming before rehearsals take a closer look at why you are going to that rehearsal in the first place. When you love the result of your hard work more than the work itself you only become fearful of making the grade, and you learn nothing—but fear.

Actors frequently ask me how to memorize their lines. I always tell them never to memorize because your memory can fail you, especially under pressure. You need to learn your lines. Make them a part of the character's experiences. You have to learn what specifically happened to your character that created the exact words the author gives you. You need to touch them every day. If you are learning a ninety-second monologue, work on it fifteen minutes. If you're not confident yet, try thirty minutes daily. If you really love it, try an hour—whatever it takes. Tape your monologue ten times in sequence and play the tape each day while traveling in your car. Don't mouth the words. Listen to the character's thought process.

Expose yourself to the learning process every day. Learning can't be forced. Learning can't be held up to a time limit. Learning must continue and develop from first read, all the way through the final performance. Learning adapts to change. The only way to truly trust yourself is to learn. Once you learn something you can't forget it, and that is when trust in yourself begins. That trust can carry you higher than you've ever been before . . . and that will refine your process and build confidence until, one day, you are totally convinced.

The fruit of hard work, discipline and tenacity is trust. Start trusting yourself as soon as possible. Trust is the antidote for fear.

Positive Energy

Positive energy is the soul driven human force that fuels our ability to overcome any obstacle to survive. Even the most depressed person I know is surrounded in positive energy. The depression itself is the only way that person can survive the emotions that seem to overwhelm them. You can safely hide behind the symptoms or the words; "I'm depressed." Others will leave you alone, which is the positive result you are seeking. You don't want to be in company when the blues hit you. You want to lock yourself in a sealed room and do whatever it takes to deal with your feelings. Exhibiting depression is the positive step towards solitude. Solitude is what you need. Others may, when conflicted, go out and binge. Alcohol, food and sex offer alternative safe havens. Still others will abuse someone they love, loathe or have never met before. Inflicting pain is the only thing that makes them feel better. The act of abuse becomes a positive impulse needed to survive their own repressed feelings. Self-destructive actions are human. The acts themselves are negative, but a positive need to survive embodies their creation.

Several years ago, I remember watching the news and they showed clips of a man acting as his own attorney. He had recently murdered several people riding home on the Long Island Railroad. He was telling the jury that those people deserved to die. He wasn't emotional. He was calm and focused. Occasionally, he would even smile or smirk at one of his perceptions towards an amazed jury. He committed horrific acts, murdering innocent commuters, and felt totally justified in his actions. There was no doubt in his mind. He felt good about it! It seemed the necessary step for his own survival. It made everyone in the courtroom sick to think of the innocent lives he tore apart on that tragic afternoon. Everyone except the person who committed the act. He was standing tall proclaiming his innocence. Society had done this to him. It was society's fault he was forced to hold on to his rage for so long. Something had to be done and he took action. He couldn't see the death, because he was fighting for his survival.

When you create a character, you must embody every action with positive energy. We, sitting outside the act, may judge you harshly, but you, the character's creator, cannot be a judge. You must create the positive impulse behind the negative act.

We all trying to survive in our own convoluted way. The act of survival is basic to human nature. Villains enjoy their villainy. Evil intent is positive, rightful action to the purveyor. Crazy people believe they make perfect sense. People strike out at others because they perceive themselves as being injured. Explore your character's life and find this positive force that links us all together as human beings. No matter how despicable your character may be, it is your job, as their creator, to make them human.

John Ford Noonan

I learned a great many things from the playwright John Ford Noonan when I was fortunate enough to work with him in the early 1990's. I directed a series of new play readings by this Irish American playwright for ten consecutive weeks in May of 1990 at the John Housman Theatre. John is a powerful writer and his characters say brutal things to each other. At first glance, they can be off-putting, but when you dig inside the material you can see each character desperately cry for help though their harsh and often merciless verbal attacks. An understanding of positive energy and the human survival instinct is essential when approaching John's work.

The following is a short example of a seemingly heartless exchange between a son and mother from John's *Club Champion's Widow*.

GLADYS: If you've got something to say than say it. I've got a big day ahead of me.

T.D.: I hope your new boyfriend treats you rotten and you end up dying alone!

GLADYS: I'm sorry for you if that's the way you really feel, but it's better than all our old lies!

T.D.: I heard everything you told Suzie.

GLADYS: I said it purposely loud for you to hear. I stank as a mother. I accept that fact. I'm not ashamed. I knew enough not to have anymore kids than you, but every second I spent with you I did my best. Of that measly fact I am very, very proud.

T.D.: Liar, liar, liar! You probably wished you'd killed me last night. That way I wouldn't haunt—

GLADYS: I will not fall to your tricks of sympathy. I will not let you walk out of here as the tragic victim. You asked for something I didn't have to give. Now hug me good-bye and get going. *(Offering arms.)*

T.D.: *(Picks up two suitcases.)* Remember! As little as I meant to you, you meant even less to me!

I think actors often make the easy choice or look for the quick solution. Anger falls into this category. "Why are you yelling?" I often ask my students this question. Nine out of ten times the reply is "Because I'm angry." "Okay, why are you angry?" Using the Noonan example the answer might be: "My mother is dishonoring my father once again by dating this new guy and I can't take it anymore—so I'm angry." "That's a little more specific but how did your mother dishonor your father?" Now there's a pause as the actor runs through the play in his mind. Finally he admits that there is no specific instance referred to in the text of the play. Now I ask, "Can you make something up?" Another pause. "Based on what you know from all the conversations in the play can you imagine, create and improvise a specific instance to back up your claim? Make up a story right now. Don't think about whether you are right or wrong just make up a specific story." The actor does this and sometimes the story is quite involved and very personal. Then I have the actor return and play the scene with that improvised incident fresh in his memory. It's no longer just anger. It's the cumulative incident of the character's life. What if he improvised another story, then another? His "anger" would now be specific and based on his experiences. His "anger" becomes his positive solution for survival.

The point is that these speeches are filled with heart. A pounding, throbbing need to survive past mistakes by lashing out in the present. When you color these words with frustration rather than anger, with quiet desperation as opposed to yelling, with accumulated hurt instead of the intention to hurt, the play opens up the family's past to the present tense moment. Everything is deepened. You care for everyone and judge the past as the villain of malevolence. Everyone who lashes out, especially to family, is coming from a positive place.

The following words are from another Noonan play, *A Critic and His Wife* but to me, they have always clearly been John's positive struggle with everything he has dealt with.

"I keep seeing the truth, I keep putting it in my sentences, but my sentences never touch my life. Why can't my life be as clear as my sentences? I'm tired of being alone. I do not want to be alone.

Additional Positives

Comedy is positive energy working through negative circumstances. You can't laugh at someone who gives up. Tenacity is the essential element.

Actors always want to know how to be funny. I love to steal George Burns' definition; "Comedy and drama are exactly the same, except comedy is a little more serious." Combine that with never-give-up-until-I-succeed determination, and you have Charlie Chaplin, Buster Keaton, Emmett Kelly and Robin Williams all rolled into one. The human spirit pointing towards success through unimaginable obstacles is funny.

Always infuse this positive energy into your character. Audiences will be drawn to your optimism. It allows them to identify. Your uncompromising spirit highlights their own daily perseverance. They need to know you will never give up, because that keeps them moving, too. You can't really cry for someone without first laughing. It's the key to opening everyone's vulnerability, and positive energy is the catalyst.

Great drama is positive energy through negative circumstances, too. In *Death of a Salesman* Willy Loman fights with all his heart the negative circumstances that a lifetime of denial has thrust in front of him. Hamlet, Othello, Macbeth, Lear, all push through the obstacles of negative circumstances to create the tragedy that eventually destroys them. We care for them through their self-destructive behavior because we identify with their positive struggle to survive. Destructive behavior is not their objective but the result of what happens to them. They have no other choice; they are overcome by events.

One of the most difficult actions for many actors is crying onstage. Sometimes, the tears won't come. I think it's because the tears become our objective. That is fear-based. You are working for a result instead of being involved with the events that surround the character. So the next logical thought becomes . . . I can't cry. I can't cry. Then . . . I can't act. I can't act becomes the logical conclusion. Crying is something that happens to you. When you feel the tears coming, there is nothing to do about it. Tears overcome you.

Some actors have it easy. You know them. They can cry at anything and often do. Many, however, abuse this gift. They fall back into their tears. The tears themselves become the drama. The tears are employed as physical proof of emotional vulnerability.

I believe tears are a blessing. As someone who has always found it difficult to cry in life, let alone on stage, I must admit some jealousy. The irony is that the few times tears have overpowered my emotions, I only remember the urge to suppress them. They usually emerge while others are present and my spirit doesn't want to reveal them to the entire world. This is a natural human phenomenon that gifted criers often ignore. They eliminate the struggle to supress. If that actor would make it their positive struggle to stop what is naturally happening to them, a deeper conflict would be created. That's what great drama is to me. A human being trying to overcome events out of their control. We can all relate. We experience it every day. We wake up and are forced to negotiate whatever life throws at us. We think it will be one thing, but it's always something else, and we must overcome our fears, emotions, expectations and yes, sometimes our tears. Everything comes without warning. Tears may overtake you and, if they do, use every fiber of your being to hold them back. This could make you cry even more, so your battle will continue, and your character's conflict will heighten with each moment of your fight.

We are constantly fighting to survive something that can't be controlled, and that fight is rooted in the positive. Make it part of your progress.

Repetition

You are afraid when you go out to audition. Your throat dries. Your voice cracks. Your hands shake. Take the first steps towards relieving your symptoms and take them often. Audition whenever possible; even if you don't want the part—especially if you don't want the part. Your nervousness is born in a lack of experience.

Think about it. Think about the things you do well. Did you do them well, I mean proficiently, the first time you tried? Even if you had a natural ability, you didn't begin with success. It's exactly the same with auditions. You have to practice. I have taught many audition classes and, if I'm in a city that is theatrically active, I insist all the students audition at least three times a week for the length of the course. If it's possible, three times in one day. Multiple auditions will deaden your nerves to the process. Some actors need more of this type of training than others do. It's different for everyone. It could take a week, a month or two years. Eventually the act of going to the audition will be fearless.

Most actors, when they begin in the business, audition once a month or once every six months. It is usually an audition they perceive as extremely important to their career. There is a considerable amount of preparation for this audition. The actor is usually ready and primed, but the audition turns into a disaster for this one reason. The actor lacks experience in the audition situation. Too much importance is attached to the result, so that is where the actor mistakenly places their focus. "I must get this job . . . I'm perfect for this part . . . I wonder what they're look-ing for?" You start sizing up everyone in the waiting room. "Oh, she's perfect for the part . . . I'm the only one with black hair in the entire room! . . . She always gets the part, and I know she'll get it now." Then, of course, just after that thought crosses your mind, they call your name. You are completely out of focus, and no matter how well prepared you are, you are blocked by your fears walking into the audition room.

This neurotic discourse must be eliminated from your process. You have to use each new audition to create positive activities that will support the time and effort you have invested in preparing for the audition.

What *not* to do:

1.) Don't start subvocalizing your monologue in an isolated cor-ner of the waiting room. If you don't know your monologue really well you shouldn't be at the audition in the first place.

2.) Don't talk to all the other actors—especially about this audi-tion. Keep your own focus.

3.) Don't question other actors that come out of the audition. Their experience is *their* experience. It has nothing to do with you.

4.) Don't anticipate or expect any result. You're here to work-out—nothing more.

5.) Don't assess how you look compared to all the other similar types sitting with you in the waiting room.

What to do!

1.) Arrive at least fifteen to thirty minutes early. Use this time to either warm-up or read over the sides of your audition and make decisions.

2.) Greet others but stay focused on the things you want to do instead of mixing with their energy.

3.) Bring something you like to read. A book or article that makes you feel good.

4.) If you must look at others think of their nervous energy as the winds of a hurricane while you remain in the eye of the storm with blue skies and calm winds.

5.) When you walk in to audition make eye contact with everyone in the room. See what you can learn about them. Introduce them to another character—yourself.

6.) Enjoy the workout of your material.

7.) When you're finished think about your next audition.

Train yourself in the audition process. When you go to auditions, work on your focus. Stay focused on your process; make that your audition objective. It's the only thing you have control over. Time, experience and repetition will diminish your fears. Your true light will be on display for all to see. Learn to refine this process with each audition and learn often!

A Paradox

On the first night of most of the audition classes I have taught over the years, I ask each student one question. If you could have three show business wishes, what would they be? I do this to get to know the spirit and focus of my students, but there is always a greater lesson. The wishes usually include some of the following: I want to be fearless in auditions. I want to get challenging roles offered to me. I want to be confident. I want to be aware of what I'm doing. I would like to have a long career with no pain involved, et cetera, et cetera. The most popular wish goes something like this: I wish to be able to choose who I work with, what, where, when I work on it and have artistic control. I think that is every artist's wish. I know it's mine, and I'm accomplishing it with each word I write in this book.

Here's the paradox. These students are enrolled in an audition class. When they create audition material, they have total artistic control. They can choose exactly what role they want to work on. They choose the audition coach (director) they want to work with. The when and where of rehearsal is completely within their control. They can even edit the material they select to increase the impact of the audition. Everything is in their control, but because it's called, "the audition" the power of creation is transferred into fear, anticipation and doubt. "Will they like it? How do you think I did? Do you think this is what they're looking for?"

When you create audition material, exert your creative power and control. Enjoy what you ultimately want from your career; The power to create. Don't sit around and wait for results. Create something that you love. Put your passion into it as if it were your own production. You become the producer, director and lead actor of this ninety-second showcase of your talents. When you get the chance to use it in an audition, think of it as an opportunity to refine and practice this evolving creation. When you go to an audition, go to rehearse your showcase. Don't go to get a result. That is up to someone else to decide. Work on all the elements you have control over. Enjoy the work for yourself. You have been granted your wish for artistic control. Audition with the power of your creations.

There Are No Rules to Creativity

A student of mine came to me with a problem to solve. She wanted to audition for a production of *Taming of the Shrew*. Bianca was her target character. She searched the text for a Bianca monologue but could only find short passages of dialogue. Bianca is not the brightest of lights and therefore speaks in short passages. Bianca is beautiful. All the men in town want her, so she lets them do the talking. Dialogue can only weaken her case. I told my student to locate a monologue from another Shakespearean ingenue approximately Bianca's age and do that monologue as if Bianca were saying it. She quickly replied that there were no other women to pull from in *Taming of the Shrew*. The monologue I'm suggesting can come from any play that Shakespeare wrote—any ingenue.

The next day, she returned with Juliet's speech to Romeo from the balcony of her bedroom window. You know . . . "O Romeo, Romeo! Wherefore art thou Romeo? Deny thy father and refuse thy name" . . . and so on. So, we went to work on this famous speech, but from Bianca's point of view. No longer was this speech from a young girl love-struck by her soul mate. Now it became Bianca's employing the exact same words as if Romeo was just another man pursuing her. To Bianca, it's no big deal that Romeo should forsake his name to pursue her love. In fact, from Bianca's point of view, it was expected. When she says, "Oh, be some other name! What's in a name? That which we call a rose, by any other name would smell as sweet!" It becomes a frivolous game for her. It's not important what you call yourself! It's only important that you love me. Life is a game, so let's play! We laughed and laughed as we poured through the speech, making connections from Bianca's witless point of view.

The day of the audition arrived. My student was well prepared. She introduced her audition saying, "Today I'm going to do Juliet's speech from *Romeo and Juliet* as if Bianca from *Taming of the Shrew* would do it. The audition hall was silent. People started exchanging glances. She began her speech as the dumb blonde, Bianca, and they started to laugh at its absurdity. They continued to laugh throughout the remainder of the monologue.

She got the part for two reasons. First, she was prepared and had a solid understanding of her character. Second, she demonstrated a creative approach to getting what she wanted. She made audition play. She made connections beyond the scope of the play she was auditioning for. She made Shakespearean connections.

When you inject creativity into your audition approach, it deepens the experience for all involved. Always remember that you have creative control over your auditions. Enjoy the process. Explore it without regard to what others will think. You will not always get the part. You may even confound some people, but the process will always be enjoyable. That, in the long run, will always serve you and your career.

Jeffery Posson

The best actor I ever worked with was a young man named
Jeffery Posson. He was totally free in his heart and mind
when he walked on stage. You could almost see an aura surround
his performance. He was charismatic whether playing a villain
or a hero. His elevated state of being was fueled by a reckless
abandoned trust in himself. He soared and relished in the flight.

I remember one performance when he was playing *Cyrano*.
He was a superhero of a Cyrano. I directed this production. It
had a five-week run, and I showed up religiously every performance for five weeks at ten fifteen to watch the fifth act. The
scene where Cyrano duels with Death is probably my favorite
scene in all literature. Anyway, this one night I arrived at my
appointed time, the lights came up. Cyrano dutifully began his
weekly gazette with Roxanne and everything was off to a brilliant
start. It was spring in Memphis, and occasionally you can get an
exceptionally hot day. As the scene progressed, Jeffrey began to
perspire profusely under the stage lights. This continued up to
the point when he draws his sword to face off with the grim reaper.
At that very moment, in the dim heated lights, his nose began to
decompose from his face. "Oh my God," I thought. "What can
he possibly do to save himself?" I wasn't even certain that Jeff
had realized the full scope of his melting dilemma.

I watched intently, and noticed subtle blocking changes, as
he became aware of his sagging protuberance. He fought on and
on with Death and his disability. First advancing on Death, then

turning slightly upstage for a secretive fix of his nostril, then another lunge. He fought and fought, never bowing to either enemy. Finally, he lay there utterly exhausted in the arms of Roxanne, who had also witnessed this fight to the death, and expired, with his nose by his side. The audience, some who only at the end noticed what had transpired, leaped to their feet and gave this magnificent Cyrano an ovation I will never forget. Jeffery got a standing ovation every performance, but never one to match this ill-fated evening.

This is what I learned from Jeffery. You never give up. Keep fighting and your ovations will come. The only thing to do is revel in the fight. Take what you are given. Create from those real elements and fate will lead you to the glory of your own creations.

The Character Leap

Jeff was also one of my acting guides when I was a graduate student at Memphis University. He taught by example what true commitment meant. He also taught a unique approach to creating character. It was purely physical and especially helpful to those who have difficulty creating character through a cognitive process. It's called a character leap and requires a complete series of isolation exercises to understand its full potential.

An isolation exercise is just as it sounds. You isolate each muscle or group of muscles from the top of your head to the tip of your toes. They are exercises that emphasize concentration and stretching over strength. Jeff would start with the face. Lift your brow . . . hold . . . now drop it. This would be repeated several times. Then lift your cheeks . . . hold . . . now drop them . . . repetitions. Extend you jaw outward . . . hold . . . now retract. Bring your jaw inward . . . hold . . . retract. Squeeze your entire face as tightly as you can . . . hold . . . now blow it out exhaling as you do. He would methodically work your neck, shoulders, arms, hands, chest, torso, hips, thighs, calves, ankles and finally your toes. It was a guided tour of your body and its avenues of expression.

He would put us in an extended position and, while we held on to it, try to get us to feel an emotional or cognitive reaction. For example, we would extend our jaw outward, then he'd say, "How do you feel changed?" The replies would come fast and furious . . . "I feel less intelligent." "I feel belligerent." "I feel like a prehistoric Neanderthal man." "I feel determined." Then we would reverse—drawing our jaws inward as far as possible. "I feel very proper." I'm more intelligent than you." I'm more sensitive, yet perplexed." Everyone would chime in, because they really did feel different. A removal from their former selves. Many people carry tension in their shoulders, so we experimented there, cataloging our impressions before moving on to another site. We spent the majority of the time on our spine. We rolled it up and back, stopping at various intervals, experiencing the subtle and not-so-subtle differences.

He made us aware that when you alter the exterior, something reacts internally, too. This happens every day of our lives. I don't need to describe what a bad hair day will do to your self-confidence. How about a zit—on your nose! A few gained or lost pounds changes everything in contemporary society. Character flows in two directions; from the inside towards an outward manifestation and from that outward manifestation inward to the soul.

Now that we were acquainted with our physical potential, he gave us the character leap exercise. I can only define it by example. You construct a monologue, physically introducing your character.

My name is Nathan Foley.

I'm from Jonesboro, Mississippi. *(Dialect change)*

I'm thirty-five years old and have been riding horses and driving cattle for twenty years . . . so my legs are slightly bowed. *(Actor makes physical adjustment)* I ride high in the saddle, always keeping my posture erect *(a slight spinal adjustment)*. I'm out in the sun at least ten to twelve hours a day, and I always wear my hat . . . so the top of my forehead is bone white while the remainder of my face and hands are sun dried. *(Actor applies Texas dirt make-up to all exposed areas)* I got in a fight when I was ten years old with a kid twice my size, and he broke my jaw. It never healed quite right, so it hangs askew forever inscribing the direction of the punch on my face *(Actor slides his jaw to the right)*

After this detailed anatomical description, the actor follows through, by leaping into their monologue while holding on to the physicality that they constructed from their own flexibility. This modified physicality created a new person, and that becomes the assumed frame of Nathan Foley's character. He speaks from the creation that automatically separates actor from character.

When Jeff was playing Cyrano, he would arrive two hours early, organize his make up and do his character leap as he applied each layer of Cyrano's pancake and prosthetic. When completed, he was Cyrano. He held on to this masterpiece of construction from fight warm-ups until the final curtain.

Next time you're having difficulty separating yourself from your character, start from the outside, and go in with a character leap.

Be Flexible

Students I coach always ask which of their monologues should go first. Try deciding when you get to the audition yourself. Go with how you feel that particular day. Predetermining the order is another fear-based ritual. If you know both monologues well, and you should, decide on the spot. This will also add more spontaneity to your introduction. Many actors rehearse their introduction as much as their monologues. This can be a big trap. It makes it too formal. When you introduce, be yourself. Be present in the room and take in the energy that surrounds you. There is good information everywhere if you have the courage to let down your guard. When you rehearse how to say your introduction, it leads toward a rehearsed monologue presentation. You've done your work, so take in today's experience. Listen to what surrounds you. Create your approach from that present tense information, and trust where your own creations lead you.

Belief

You have to believe and know in your heart that what you aspire to is out there. You need to release the earthly trappings of when, where, how and especially what time it will arrive. You just have to know and get to work—joyfully. Immerse your energy into the work itself. A vision for your future is sentient. Once you've clearly seen it you have to stop looking for its appearance. It's there, so let it be. It's like taking a long journey in a car. You remember when you were a child you kept repeating, "Are we there yet?" the trip always took forever because we looked for our destination at every mile marker. One trip my father gave my sister and me a game. It was a large bingo card, but instead of numbers in each square, there were state license plates. The entire trip, my sister and I searched every car for their license plate origin. I think my sister got bingo twenty-five miles from our destination point. She always won. Anyway, it was the fastest trip we ever took, because we did the work of the game. Getting there was actually the biggest surprise.

Our own energy can be our greatest asset or our biggest liability. It's a catch-22. Just like joining Actor's Equity Association. You know; you can't get an audition unless you are a member of the union. And you can't be member of the union unless you are offered a union job. Yet, people join AEA every day. Somehow it just happens. The right opportunity presents itself.

For the longest time I had difficulty establishing long-term relationships with the opposite sex. I always knew, deep in my soul, there was a perfect compliment for me, someone to understand and love me unconditionally. I had this vision. I also had a great propensity for falling in love. I did—many times. But after a period of time, usually two and a half years, something would always grow dim. I would realize this was not the woman of my vision. This repeated itself for too many years. I'm sure my shortcomings were just as obvious to all who shared this journey to my vision.

One day, at a time when I wasn't even searching, this woman entered my life. I knew it was her, but I could not approach. I was married at the time and committed to making it work even though the marriage wasn't fulfilling my expectations. Nothing, not even the realization of my vision, could make me stray from my commitment. It was my second marriage and my tenacity was solid. Many months passed and, as fate would have it, my wife asked me for a divorce. I was devastated. I had put my vision aside to tend to my commitment, and the marriage pushed me away.

I remember sitting in a rented room doing the "I Ching" and my pennies tossed me to the chapter entitled, "Stagnant." I laughed and cried at the same time. The pond of my life was motionless. It was completely quiet, but that stillness enabled me to hear a voice that most assuredly emanated from my abandoned vision.

I am happy to tell you that twelve years later, one Chinese cycle, by the way, I am more in love with Denise than when she first walked into my life. You wouldn't be reading this if it weren't for her. She supports, encourages, soothes, comforts and inspires me every day . . . exactly as my vision had led me to believe.

I have a similar vision for my career. I know what I want. I know exactly what it looks like. I haven't found it yet, but each day I commit myself to the page and do the work. It doesn't always fulfill my expectations, but my tenacity is solid. I work to spend less energy looking, expecting and anticipating the time of arrival. It will appear. I know it. Just like Denise, it will appear. I also know exactly when it will arrive. Just like Denise. When I stop looking and trust my vision. It's that energy of anticipation that keeps it at bay. The process is simple, yet infinitely complicated. Believe in your visions and do the work—every day.

Surviving Bad Directors

The mark of an accomplished actor is one who can survive a bad director. We all need direction, encouragement, security, empathy, inspiration and a good editor. A director can provide all of the above and more. Directors can also be completely lost in the sea of their own visions. A director can be blind. A director can be antithetical to the entire process.

You, as the actor, must make decisions that benefit you. You must survive. The play can fail. All the actors around you may flounder, but somehow you must survive. There is a way to turn any negative around into a positive. You may not always be able to clear that path, but you must believe the potential is present. The minute you fall back into self-pity you become part of the problem and lose your power of solution. Don't retreat into mediocrity for anyone. Continue to push through. The only mistake you can make in this situation is to surrender.

The Non-Communicative Director

This person has difficulty expressing ideas and opinions. They seem involved in every aspect of the production but the actor's process. They generally give very little, if any, feedback to the actors. They don't seem connected to the reality you are trying to create. It doesn't seem like this director wants to get down in the trenches with you to discover anything. The creative process seems to become a vacuum that you are trapped in with no fresh air to breathe and few points of reference.

This director's strength usually lies in the production's visuals, pictures and atmosphere. You ask this director if they liked what you did, and they say, "Yes, but try it another way." You comply and receive no feedback. You ask again and get a similar reply. "Try it another way." You comply and get the same results. Your frustration is now piqued because you have lost all frame of reference. This is where the actor makes the mistake of surrender. Don't do it. Don't retreat. Take a larger look at your director's strength—the visuals. What do these visuals say about your character and the issues of your dilemma? They say a picture is worth a thousand words, so write about what you see. Now, here's the difficult part. Make your own decisions. If you don't decide, nothing will happen. Believe in your decisions. Listen and commit to what goes on around you. Allow those elements to lead you to your next decision. Don't wait for approval. Don't expect feedback. Be part of the solution through decision making.

Warning: Don't observe the results of your decisions.

Don't put your energy outside of your own character and judge. Don't try to be your own director—trust how your character reacts. Stay in character.

The Director Who Directs Everything

When I first began to direct, I was this director. I felt responsible for every gesture, intonation, expression and action on stage. My script was cramped with stage directions. I thought since the artistic success of the play was my responsibility I had to come up with every solution. I thought theatre was about me, the director. Over thirty years of directing has taught me the opposite. I've found that, when I surround myself with artists who are as or more creative than myself, I can sit back and be the editor of everyone's brilliance. I can better construct my vision by channeling through everyone else's creativity. I need to work with actors and designers that are able to create something I don't know about the play and with artists who spark my imagination rather than those who live comfortably within its limitations. I admit all of this to make you aware of how well I know this director. Their behavior is manifested by insecurity. Their intentions are noble—all for the benefit of the play but, if the ideas don't spring from them, insecurity creeps into the picture. A good idea is often rejected because the director is not the source. Actors can become overtly defensive to this excessive control, and then battle lines are drawn.

Please remember the issue here is insecurity. Turn it around to your favor. You can't change this director's resolve. Only time and experience will do that. Make this director believe your ideas; your decisions have emerged from the director's visions. "You know, you said this in rehearsal yesterday, and it really got me thinking, so I came up with this." Or, "I read that rehearsal article you gave the cast, and I see what you're doing, so I'm going to try this . . . thanks!" Put your decisions in the director's terms and build a relationship. Now, you still may be forced to do something you don't totally agree with, but it will always be more effective born in an atmosphere of collaboration as opposed to confrontation. Confrontation will end all negotiations with this insecure director.

If you can't stand this person, find a way to survive, then make the decision not to work with them again. As long as you are not insecure, you will survive this director.

The Histrionic Screamer

There comes a point in any relationship when you must state what you will or will not tolerate. You can't accept abuse indefinitely. You can swallow it, hold things deep within yourself but at some point it will manifest. If you hold too long you will become a victim. It will make you sick.

When this director enters your life you must face the challenge. Don't retain anger, hurt and resentment because that will make you part of the problem. One day, you will erupt catapulting your rage in many directions. Identification of the actual problem will be impossible and you will now be perceived as the irrational force. Don't let this happen!

The histrionic screamer treats all actors alike. Don't be like the other actors. Separate yourself. Ask for a private conference to calmly express your feelings. Patiently set your guidelines for communication. "This may be your natural way of working, but it doesn't work for me. It stifles my trust and closes down my imagination. Please do not raise your voice to me. You have a great deal to offer, but I cannot accept your method of delivery—especially with others present." Once you set your creative guidelines, stick to them. Don't be intimidated or fearful. Your own fear will most certainly block every creative instinct you possess. Stand up for yourself as an artist. The only mistake you can make in this situation is to be afraid . . . So don't be afraid to extricate yourself if that is your only alternative.

The Early Career-or
Inexperienced Director

This is a tenuous topic, because it is driven by point of view. You, with your many years of experience in theatre, may judge someone's actions as inexperienced, while another actor may be quite taken with the director's enthusiasm, passion and eye for the smallest detail. I have worked with actors who felt themselves superior to my abilities. It was difficult, but not impossible as long as they didn't make a show of their experience. When an actor deliberately and publicly contradicts their director, communication becomes an exposed battleground. We are all fearful of going into battle, so the creative process gets put on hold while everyone awaits a resolution. Confrontation places pallor upon the entire process.

The worst creative experience I've had was at the Syracuse Stage Company. It was a production of a musical entitled: "Closer than Ever." The irony of the title still makes me chuckle or cringe occasionally until this day. I was brought into the process by accident. The original director had become ill. I did not cast the show or collaborate on any of its visual concepts. I was the foreigner who was thrust into the process to make these established concepts succeed. All began as it should, on an upbeat note. By the end of the first week of rehearsal we were clearly on the same track. Everything changed after I had dinner early the following week with one of the two actresses in the cast. As we chatted between courses I was asked what my next project was. I openly admitted I was going to a Cleveland community theatre to direct a production of Harry Chapin's "Lies and Legends." I also added that it was my first show as the new artistic director of that theatre. There was a brief silence. The tone of our conversation changed after I had openly shared this information. Then the tone of the rehearsals began to change until I was being challenged by three of the four actors on almost every idea I would try to inject into the process. Something had happened. The actress I shared dinner with had recently been nominated for a Tony award and now felt she was working with an early career "community theatre director." She passed this information on to the other cast members and the creative process was completely altered. The cast began to confront every choice I made—not privately, but publicly in front of all present in the rehearsal hall.

Now my job was to make this show work. I was brought in on short notice for that one purpose. My first instinct was to fire those three actors who had closed me out of the process but we were opening in six days. That solution would not have served the production. I went to the artistic director, discussed my dilemma and created this solution. I would sit in rehearsals, watch the run throughs and take my notes. We would then take a break. During that recess I would give my notes to the choreographer. The actors would reassemble, get the notes from the choreographer and work on the changes. The cast was told by the artistic director that the choreographer was taking over the direction of the play but they were not informed that he was acting as my surrogate. The confrontation ended, the creative process was reignited and the show was a huge success. The greatest irony of "Closer the Ever" was the fact that the cast never realized that they were executing my direction. I was able to rescue the creative process by removing myself from the battleground. It was a horrifying experience. I would never do it again but, in this situation, eliminating the confrontation was the most creative solution.

If you are an experienced actor, the early career director has already exhibited wisdom by casting you. Let this action alone temper any frustrations that may arise during the process. I was fortunate to have several master actors subtly guide me through some sophomoric instincts.

In the early eighties I worked with a veteran English actor named Paul Lee. We became great friends. My first acting assignment at the Cleveland Play House was in a play called "Appear and Show Cause." Paul and I were both minor characters in it and consequently spent hours together talking about theatre backstage. I think Paul fell in love with my open passion for theatre and especially directing. He took me under his wing. Our second season we were teamed up to work on a production of "The Potsdam Quartet" only this time I was the director. I remember being quite intimidated by the cast. The Cleveland Play House, at that time, was one of the last remaining true repertory theatres left in the United States. Some of the actors had been in this same company for over twenty years. They knew their craft and had a loyalty and respect for each other's tenure. Several actors of this experienced group, including Paul, were in "Potsdam." I felt like a kid. I was thirty-three going on seventeen. I think I also had a lot to prove so I wanted to "take control."

This was the wrong approach. My friend Paul pulled me aside into my small office after the third or fourth rehearsal. He wanted a private talk. "Don't decide everything so quickly," he said. "Give us a chance to feel something for these characters ourselves. We've been doing this for quite a while now and you're forcing our decisions before we know who we are." " But I know what will work. Why waste time? Why not get right to it? What's the problem? "The problem is," my patient mentor retorted, "the problem is that you are not going to be up on that stage with us each night so *we* have to find our own way. Let us search for a while and *then* try to bring our wanderings together. Let us create then edit our creations into your vision."

This was the beginning and it was because Paul collaborated with me instead of confronting me in front of the others. I still didn't learn my lesson completely because I had so much to learn but Paul began a process for change through creative encouragement. I began to realize that the process was not all about me. I saw, for the first time, I think, that my job as director was to listen more than talk. Paul Lee took an early career director and gently cleared a new path for him. Instead of closing me off he opened up my imagination by allowing me to trust the imagination of the actor as much as my own. Paul has been dead for almost fifteen years now and I can still hear his laughter with each stroke of my pen. Thanks, Paul. I wouldn't be who I am if it weren't for you.

Rehearsals are delicate and need to be a safe haven for all in the room. Everyone is vulnerable. Consequently considerate, supportive, patient and positive actions are the only protection for exposed parts. Situations arise that can alter the chemistry of the ensemble and, although it's not the actor's job to create an atmosphere for free expression, the early career director needs to be nurtured rather than bullied towards an obvious creative choice. Once again, I urge full disclosure through the device of a private conference. Protecting the creative process will most directly benefit your needs. When working with an early career director, be a leader for everyone; especially the less experienced. Let your own wisdom lead you towards a positive, nurturing process. Prove you have earned your veteran stripes without making a show of it. This could be a turning point for your creative process and you might just help a few others, along with the art form itself. We all started somewhere, and you can be certain you wouldn't be in this situation if several artists along the way didn't give you the benefit of their experience.

The Incompetent Director

This director is not difficult to identify. The auditions are your first clue. Callbacks can confirm any suspicions. Watch, listen, and research actors who have experience with this director. You must decide for yourself. What do you want to get out of this project? Do you want exposure? Is this a great role that you have always wanted to play? Will doing this project enable you to get a foot in the door? You are clearly not going to get a creative experience, so if that's your objective, look for another opportunity. Trust your instincts and get out before you get involved.

If you're in a room with several other actors and you're the most creative person there . . . it's time to go to another room.

A Workbook of Clues

There is a wonderful book which has nothing to do with acting that can be an invaluable resource for the actor. The book is entitled *You Can Heal Your Life* by Louise Hay. This book makes direct connections between human emotion and its physical manifestations. The premise is simply that there is a specific emotional connection to every physical ailment the human body suffers. If we can adjust our emotional instincts we can heal ourselves. Let me list a couple of examples from this insightful book. (see page 129)

Just about every ailment known to man is listed in the middle section of this book. I chose ailments that often strike the characters we play onstage. When your character has a physical infirmity, disability or injures a specific part of their anatomy, this book will offer clues to the emotional source.

Cyrano just flashed into my thoughts and I turn to "Nose" in Louise Hay's book. "Nose represents self-recognition. I recognize my own intuitive ability." Now if that's not Cyrano I don't know what is! Next, Brick from "Cat on a Hot Tin Roof" comes to mind. He has a broken ankle. "Ankle represents inflexibility and guilt. Ankles represent the ability to receive pleasure." Brick is also an alcoholic so turn to the previous page and look up the probable cause for yourself. Let's take one more example from the same play. Big Daddy is dying of cancer. Locate the source of Big Daddy's pain. These are all clues that bring a more specific problem to light that are derived from the symptoms the playwright has worked into your character.

You can use it in your life. Discover the probable cause of your friends, family members or your own medical problems. It even provides council towards a solution. Buy this book, and use it as resource. It's not always the answer, but it can provide insights. There is a direct connection between deep inner emotion and serious physical manifestation for yourself and your character's lives. Research all you can. Be creative in every aspect of building your character.

This is the part of acting that must be joyful—looking deeper. Create methods for discovery based on each individual character you are challenged with. When I teach an introduction to acting class each year we always get to the class where I ask each student to compose a character study; to write a timeline narrative of their character's life. Generally the first question is: "How long do they have to be?" We all want to finish. I occasionally find myself flipping towards the remainder of this book to count how many more things my editor wants me to re-write before I finish. This is our training; to finish. If we really want to create we have to de-program this thought out of our mind. Finishing is actually the enemy because the joy of the process is what truly gives us the opportunity to create. The best writing I ever do occurs when I just get completely lost in extracting the story that, for some reason, I must tell. When you lose track of time it is always because you are immersed in process. You have to enjoy getting lost. It's the journey of discovery that leads to great creation. Louise Hay is just one of the infinite number of creative paths towards understanding your character's deepest motives. Seek out your own, and if you can't get lost in the process, seek out something in your life that you can get lost in.

Problem	Probable Cause	New Thought Pattern
Alcoholism	What's the use? Feeling of futility, guilt, self-rejection	I live in the now. Each moment is new. I choose to see my self worth. I love and approve of myself.
Arthritis	Feeling unloved. Criticism, resentment.	I am love. I now choose to love and approve of myself. I see others with love.
Arthritic fingers	A desire to punish. Blame. Feeling victimized.	I see with love and understanding. I hold all my experiences up to the light of love.
High blood pressure	Long-standing emotional problem not solved.	I joyously release the past. I am at peace.
Cancer	Deep hurt. Long-standing resentment. Deep secret or grief eating away at the self. Carrying hatreds. What's the use?	I lovingly forgive and release all of the past. I choose to fill my world with joy. I love and approve of myself.
Back problems		
Lower	Fear of money. Lack of financial support	I trust the process of life. All I need is always taken care of. I am safe.
Middle	Guilt. Stuck in all that stuff back there. "Get off my back."	I release the past. I am free to move forward with love in my heart.
Upper	Lack of emotional support. Feeling unloved. Holding back love.	I love and approve of myself. Life supports and loves me.

The Power of the Script

I once coached a wonderful actress. She was out of town doing a production of *Lend Me a Tenor*, the great Ken Ludwig farce. I got a call one evening, because she had a dilemma. She was playing Maria and in rehearsal, her Tito would raise his arm to her as if to strike. This was distressing at the time and a bit intimidating because this particular Tito had played the role in two other productions. She felt this threat of violence was out of character but didn't feel it was her place to deliver this information. The director had made no comment as well.

I asked her if she used the power of the script. She seemed confused by this reply, so I asked her another question. Does it say in the script that Tito strikes Maria? Her answer was an immediate "No." Then why is your character so thrown by this impotent gesture of violence? If he can't really hit you, what are you afraid of? The fact that he can't strike you should empower your character. The next time he raises his arm, stand up to him. Dare him to strike. Use the power of the script to put Tito in his proper place.

Jane Meadows did this all the time in "The Honeymooners." Ralph would constantly threaten violence. She would stand there; hands on hips, with her jaw wide open because she knew he couldn't hit her. It wasn't in the script! This actually turned the entire situation around and gave Alice the power over Ralph. Maria has the same advantage with Tito.

The next rehearsal she stood up to Tito's threat. The twice-played Tito was so taken back, so completely disarmed that he never raised his arm to her again. He also gained a new respect for Maria as well as the actress playing her.

What's not in the script can also have as much power as what is. Using my *"Lend me a Tenor"* example you can clearly see *that's* what empowers Maria to stand up to any of Tito's bullying. The author would have notated the action of striking Maria if he intended Tito to demonstrate his dominance. If the actor mistakenly takes this liberty as our "experienced Tito" did, find a creative counter of your own invention. There is no confrontation in the script. What isn't there becomes just as powerful as what is.

The script is your greatest behavioral ally. Use it religiously in developing your approach and creating solutions for yourself and your character. The more you reinforce the author's intentions the closer you become to the character born in the playwright's mind. The critical clues that separate artist from character are in the script. Use it as your guideline. Create from there and see where it leads you.

The Full Stretch

When I'm looking for a truth inside me that I don't hold in my center, when I'm searching for something that feels new and different or when I'm trying to learn anything unfamiliar, I stretch myself to the extreme limits of the search. I believe you must go beyond what you are looking for in order to settle back into the center of your exploration's core. When you take a rubber band and expand it to the limits in every direction without snapping its elasticity, and release the rubber band, its center will be bigger. If you strain too far it will snap and turn into something all together different. It will damage the original form forever.

I think education, especially the process of learning, to an actor, is similar. When you explore, it must be with reckless abandon. You must strive to go beyond your own limitations as well as those others have set for you—without snapping. Trust your collaborators to keep you safe. If you intuitively feel they are irresponsible, pull back to where you feel protected. When you sense you are being nurtured and guided through these difficult stretches, you should trust those instincts. Don't be bullied by someone who is stretching you for his or her own purposes. This process is all about you, so make certain you get support you can trust from your collaborators.

How many times have you gotten a direction like, "Give me a little more." Then you comply. The next day you are asked to do still more and you do. The following day, there is another request and you snap. You are confused. You have been delivering more with each direction. What more can you do? What more can they want? Now, everyone is frustrated.

When you are asked to expand your reach, go to its limits as your first instinct. Don't creep up on it. Seize an opportunity for growth and take it all the way. Now, the next direction will be to ease or fall back into what you just discovered. This is better for everyone. It develops an environment that breeds creativity.

When I feel you are willing to take a chance or risk a boundary you have arbitrarily set for yourself it motivates me to return the effort. Whether you succeed or fail is unimportant because a channel of communication and trust is opened in the process. I remember standing on the edge of a diving board for the first time when I was a child. My father was just below and in front of me with his arms extended, treading water, ready to secure the safety of my first dive. I wanted to jump. I wanted to go where I hadn't gone before; I wanted to test my limits. I back away and go sit by my mother afraid of the consequences. I don't take that leap of faith. I protect myself. I never realized until right this second how my father must have felt and how that one simple moment of panic on my part defined much of our relationship for years to come. I'm sure he was hurt that I didn't trust his open arms. I didn't mean to but I was closing down an avenue for trust that would have otherwise opened up a new understanding and basis for creativity in both of us.

While you are growing, stretch all the way. It will feel so good, as long as you're not worried about making a mistake by going too far. Trust your collaborators to keep you from snapping. You will always learn more from a full stretch . . . and your willingness will directly affect the entire creative process.

A Neat Little Package

Keep your audition monologues short. No less than a minute and no longer than ninety seconds. Many actors, especially those coming out of college, have two and a half or three-minute monologues. I think this is counter-productive for several reasons. First, you usually only have two. That is six minutes of material and you are only putting two colors on your palate. This approach comes from the old contrasting monologue days. This got you into college, but it's not as relevant in the professional world. You may find a need for more subtle colors and textures as you search for a paying job; monologues that more specifically modify different notes in your range, rather than just the opposite ends of the spectrum. I think a successful combination for an actor who wants to do both classical and contemporary theatre might be the following: Two dramatic monologues (one contemporary and one classical), two comic monologues (one contemporary and one classical) one monologue that is created from a source outside the theatre i.e. a novel, a film, an interview from a magazine, a trial manuscript or anything else you might find that excites your imagination. I've even had a student who constructed an audition monologue from a greeting card! The point is it should be yours. No one else could possibly duplicate your idea. Also look for contrast or shadings within your choices. If you choose two comic monologues make one black comedy, or absurdist, or slapstick, or frivolous or farcical. Each time you select what to do make certain that you feel a spiritual connection to the material.

When your audition monologues are between sixty and ninety seconds, you still have six minutes of material, but you now have five different selections to choose from.

Secondly, I don't see the advantage of dragging a monologue out for three minutes. Most casting directors will tell you they make their decisions within the first fifteen seconds. I've seen many actors lose a job they have won by prolonging their monologue. Here's how it may go in the casting director's mind as you present your audition. The first fifteen seconds: "Oh, very nice. Good vocal. Good human connection." The next fifteen seconds: "She moves very well. Nice range." The next fifteen seconds: "Good monologue selection. The actor is well-prepared for this audition." The next thirty seconds: "Perfect yes, this is the one!" The next thirty seconds: "Oh, I see what she is doing. This is not exactly what I thought. "The next thirty seconds: "No, no. I was wrong. I don't see where she is going." The final thirty seconds: "This is too much. When will this be over." Now, I'm not saying it always goes like this, but often does. What if her monologue ended at one minute and fifteen seconds when our hypothetical casting director loved her? What's the worst thing that could happen? They could say, "That was terrific. Do you have anything else?" That is actually the best thing that can happen to you in an audition. You know they're interested and you're sure you've made a good impression. Now, with your new multiple monologue approach, your next line is, "yes, I have four more. What would you like to see?" the casting director has an opportunity to be impressed once more by the completeness of your preparation.

Finally, if you're not what they're looking for, and they know that immediately, they will respect you more if you're out in seventy-five seconds rather than sitting through three full minutes. You may not be right for this project, but you have a better chance of being remembered for future projects if you don't waste their time.

A finely crafted and edited monologue should have an impacting beginning. It should engage the listener in the present tense of your character's dilemma. It should impact them in a way that draws them to you. There needs to be a clear development. Most good audition monologues are about a character dealing with one obstacle. A clear picture is developed as the monologue progresses and the character is altered somehow by this progression. Most importantly it needs a definite ending. Make sure your character has said their final word on the subject. A good audition monologue doesn't end when the actor stops talking, only when your character has completed their thought.

Make each of your five audition selections a neat little package. Give yourself and the people trying to cast you more options at each audition.

Looking Better When You're Ill

Next time you are sick and you have to drag yourself to an important audition, rehearsal or meeting, change your approach. Most of us, upon entering the room will say something like, "I have a bad cold, so I can't do this one part of the monologue that requires my full voice." Singers inevitably must say, "I'm doing my song an octave lower today, because I have a respiratory infection." These statements are true, but they can come off sounding like an excuse.

Next time, when you enter the room, try saying something like, "I'd shake your hand but I'm not feeling well today." This is a thoughtful way to highlight your situation. You are being considerate, and consideration will trigger the empathy you desire much more effectively than any excuse. It also quietly announces you are ready to do anything but pass your misfortune to them. I like you already. Now push though your obstacle with courage, and you just might win the day for yourself.

Finding a Needle in a Haystack

When you look for audition monologues, don't go to monologue books. You want to find material that is all your own. Everyone goes to monologue books because it's easy. Here are two ways to separate yourself from the pack.

Every time you see a play or film, fill out a three by five index card that includes title, author, date of performance and your impression of the experience. When you see a character you would be perfect for, or would love to explore, make a special notation. Place these special cards in a box and let them accumulate. They are ideas for audition material. After time, you will be able to file them in categories such as, classical, comedies, dramas and so on. Now when you need a monologue you go to your file of passions. This takes time to develop but it can be an invaluable resource.

While waiting for your file to bulk up, try trusting your psychic instincts for an inspired monologue selection. Call Samuel French, Inc. or Dramatists Play Service, and have them mail you one of their play catalogs. Both are located in Manhattan and both should mail you their complete catalog of plays at no cost. I'm certain you can also gain complete access through the Internet. Now, go to the listings by title and make a list of every play that sparks your interest. You could end up with a list of over one hundred titles. Don't think about it beyond the fact that you are instinctively drawn to the title. Next, look up each of the selected titles and read the play's description. When you read something about a character or play scenario that makes a deeper instinctual connection, add that to a new list. Give each new addition a ranking of one to ten. Finally, pick your five to ten highest ranked plays and order them. Out of these plays you may just discover your needle in a haystack.

Finding an audition monologue can be a frustrating experience, because you are looking for a quick result. Don't take the well-traveled road. Do your research and trust your instincts. Audition material is a calling card that leaves an impression. Make it your own.

The Mini-Lesson

When I first started to teach *Acting By Mistake* in New York at the Mint Theatre Company, I would give a one-hour mini-lesson. No one had ever heard of me but people were intrigued by the title of the course. In this hour, I would, with some detail, outline the basic principles of my approach. I would always take one or two students from the audience and have them perform one of their audition monologues. I would either identify one of their protections or have them make some other adjustment based on a principle of *Acting By Mistake*. There would always be a noticeable improvement on the spot. The mini-class would be impressed by this sudden change. Consequently, I never had difficulty filling my class. Next, I would ask for questions and, inevitably, one of my guests would raise a hand and say, "Is this it?" I would reply, "Well, yes. These are many of the things we will work with during the ten weeks of the class." There would usually be a slight pause before they retorted back, "If I've heard the entire content here today, why should I spend the money to take the class?"

You can intellectually understand the basic principles discussed in this book. Being able to execute your understanding is an entirely different challenge. Don't try to do everything at once. Extract the ideas one at a time. Spend as much time as it takes to ingrain them into your developing process. Now go on to something else. After you're finished go back and spend a day with what came before. Now go on to something new. Go back again and revisit the two concepts that came before. Re-work your discoveries until they become instinctual.

You can buy a new pair of jeans that look great but they are never comfortable—until you spend some time in them.

You can clearly comprehend that sub-vocalizing your next line is not the most creative activity, but stopping the process will take time and practice. You can plainly see that listening to yourself and staying in the moment of your character's life are impossible to do simultaneously, but refining methods that break this habit you've developed over years of training will require careful observation, patience and time. This book and the one-hour mini-lesson have one thing in common. They are the first step of a long journey. Many people have taken my class several times, not because they are slow, or can't understand the basic premise, but because it takes hard work, patience and tenacity to develop trust in yourself.

I know for certain that, one day, I will remove expectation, anticipation and fear from my actions. I will trust the universe that has created me to manifest my dreams and I will feel totally blessed no matter what the outcome. I've known this intellectually for several years, but I'm still doing the day-to-day practice rituals as I patiently await their arrival. Stay focused on the work. That is how you complete the course. It takes time. There's no such thing as a mini-lesson.

Afterword

I want this to be a practical guide to developing a healthy approach to an art form that requires healthy practitioners. I have worked with many inspiring artists in my career and the ones I remember most fondly possessed a great joy located at the center of their process. They always found a way to make things work. No anger. No demands. No tantrums. No manipulation. No power plays. I could go on forever listing what they didn't do, but what they all had in common was a comfort with themselves, and a love of process.

I want to find a place, call them all close and absorb their contentment. This would be a relaxed space; open. People listen and their creative thoughts are spun by what they hear. We all love a dilemma. The challenge of its solution is what brings us together. People suggest the absurd. It's met by deserved laughter. In the calm that follows, we begin to create. I can listen all day without saying a word, then, all at once, my mind is enlightened not with the solution, but with a question that embodies the entire afternoon of thought. We laugh again. This is the key element. It liberates age and aberates time. We have no concern for time. We are lost in this process and safe.

I wish this for everyone. It's not a dream. I have experienced moments like this, as I'm sure many of you have. Over thirty years of work has accumulated at least three years of bliss. I'm blessed for that, but not satisfied. I want it all the time and believe it will happen. I have no idea when, although I want it tomorrow. I have no idea where, but I hope it's around the corner. I'm going to keep making mistakes until I figure it out. I'm going to listen, create and see where it leads me.